UNIQUE CHALLENGES OF AFRICAN AMERICAN PASTORS

DR. TERRY L. WEEMS

Unique Challenges of African American Pastors

Copyright © 2007 2017 Dr. Terry L. Weems
All rights reserved.

World rights reserved. No part of this publication may be stored in a retrieval system, transmitted, or reproduced in any way, including but not limited to photocopy, photograph, magnetic or other record, without prior agreement and written permission of the author

ISBN: 1-931527-75-X

TABLE OF CONTENTS

TABLE OF CONTENTS..i

BOOK DEDICATION..ii

ABSTRACT...iii

NOTE ON TERMINOLOGY..iv

Chapters

Page

1. HISTORY OF THE AFRICAN AMERICAN CHURCH IN THE UNITED STATES..1

2. THEOLOGICAL AND THEORETICAL VIEWPOINTS...17

3. LITERARY REVIEW..27

4. THE AUTHOR'S RESEARCH..50

5. SUGGESTED MINISTRY BASED ON THE UNIQUE CHALLENGES..67

6. CONCLUSION...85

Appendix

1. SURVEY FORM FOR PASTORS..................................95

2. SURVEY FORM FOR CLASS.......................................100

SELECTED BIBLIOGRAPHY...105

BOOK DEDICATION

This book project is humbly dedicated to my immediate family; Sherry, T.J, and the late J.T. who supported me wholeheartedly allowing me the freedom to spend countless days and nights working on this project.

Secondly, this project would have never been completed without the staff of New Life Fellowship. The work of Pastor Tasha Dillon, Min. Darlene Kennedy, Sis. Theatrice Watts, and Sis. Belinda Matthews was indispensable to the compilation of the material and final touches.

Also, my church family, who allowed me to research, teach, preach, and fine-tune most of this material at their expense, is awesome.

Finally, to all of the pastors, ministers, and New Life Fellowship School of Ministry students who participated in focus groups, completed surveys, and allowed me the privilege of teaching this material, I am forever indebted.

ABSTRACT

Title: A Discovery of the *Unique Challenges of African American Pastors*, which also gives distinct attention to and addresses pastors of small churches in the south

Abstract: It is indisputable that there are different races of people and cultures in our country. It is undeniable that different churches have different focuses or emphasis. But are there different challenges that are faced by African American pastors, particularly in the South, as opposed to other pastors. This paper seeks to answer this question and to highlight such challenges.

This study begins with the history of how the African American church began in the South and follows its development, pausing along the way to examine key issues that still impact the African American church and pastor of today. The book also references past studies along with including survey information, interviews, etc. from this author to determine differences between those pastoring in predominately white congregations as opposed to those pastoring in predominately African American congregations. Also, there are recommendations made as to how an African American pastor of a small church in the South can minister effectively in respect to the unique challenges he or she may face.

NOTE ON TERMINOLOGY

Based on current literature and the twenty-first century era in which we now live, most readers may find themselves most comfortable with the term "African American" to denote the community under discussion in this dissertation. Although this may not be true for all, it will be typically true for most people of today. However, as the reader approaches this work, it must be noted that a variety of terms have been used over time. Terms such as Negro race, black American or black church, or African American or African American church, have all been used at different points in history.

This current author will use a variety of these terms throughout the paper. Depending upon the time period under discussion or the context, one term may be preferred over the other. In a number of cases, these terms will be used in the context of a direct quote from a previous author. Regardless of which term is used, the reference point will always go back to the community under discussion.

Finally, in the literary review of chapter three, the term "nigger" is used. This use is a direct quote from the book, *The Journal of a Southern Pastor*. The quotation is inserted as a point of historical fact and is not intended to arouse any negative feelings on the part of those who read this work.

CHAPTER 1

HISTORY OF THE AFRICAN AMERICAN CHURCH IN THE UNITED STATES

The purpose of this first chapter is to show the effect of the beginnings of the African American church on its present-day pastoral leadership and church congregations. In studying any phase of the character and the development of the social and cultural life of the Negro in the United States, one must recognize from the beginning that because of the manner in which the Negroes were captured in Africa and enslaved, they were practically stripped of their social heritage.[1] Our study will go back to the time in which African Americans were brought to the United States, and we will examine how the church developed among this group of people. The uprooting of

---

[1] Franklin E. Frazier, *The Negro Church in America*, (New York: Schocken Books, 1973), 1.

Negroes and the transportation of them to an alien land undoubtedly had a shattering effect upon their lives.[2] In destroying their traditional culture and in breaking up their social organization, slavery deprived them of their accustomed orientation towards the world.[3]

Contrary to early misconceptions and still popularly held beliefs concerning the primitiveness of African religions, the peoples from which the slaves were drawn possessed developed systems of religious beliefs concerning their place in nature and in society.[4] In the crisis which they experienced the enslaved Negroes appealed to their ancestors and their gods. But their ancestors and their gods were unable to help them. Some slaves committed suicide during the 'middle passage' while others sought the same means of escape from bondage in the new environment.[5] The vast majority of the slaves submitted to their fate, and in their confusion and bewilderment sought a meaning for their existence in the new white man's world.[6] The new orientation to the world was provided by Christianity as communicated to the slaves by their white masters.

Naturally, those elements among the slaves who worked and lived in close association with the whites were more influenced by Christian teachings and practices than the

---

[2] Ibid., 9.
[3] Ibid.
[4] Ibid.
[5] Ibid., 10.
[6] Franklin, *The Negro Church in America*, 9.

slaves who had few contacts with the whites.[7]

All of the above play a major role in the mindset of African Americans during this era of African American church history. In this introductory chapter, we will take a look at the major African American denominations, which will include the Baptist, Methodist, and the Pentecostal groups, and show how they developed. Of these groups, the oldest and most prominent institutional paradigms of Christianity in black America are, namely, the African Methodist Episcopal Church and the National Baptist Convention, U.S.A., Inc.[8] The author's attempt will not be to give all the details of each group but rather to give a snapshot of information that will serve as a basis to make the conclusions that the modern day leader in the African American church is, in some way, having to still wrestle with issues that were brought on by the past. Those issues having to be dealt with are: a) How the African American church sees itself; b) How the church is viewed by others in America; and c) How the leaders of today are impacted by the decisions, preaching and leadership of the early leaders.

As we attempt to go back and trace the early days of the African American Church in the United States, there are limited sources to view for this task. In the book, *The Black Church in America*, Clifton F. Brown's statement is enlightening.

---

[7] Ibid., 10.

[8] Peter J. Paris, *The Social Teaching of the Black Churches*, (Philadelphia: Fortress Press, 1985), xi.

The foundation of black religion in America, conceived as it was against a background of slavery and segregation, provided the black man with the opportunity to be free while still in chains. Black religion produced a gospel of future hope and a theology of the suffering servant. Yet black religion was also a protest movement--a protest against a system and a society that was deliberately designed to demean the dignity of a segment of God's creation.[9]

This particular book also argues that because of the past, there is also a differentiation of the black church that was formed as it relates to residency and class.

The book, *The Negro Church in America* has a similar flow of thought and history as *The Black Church in America*, although it has a different author. The author of this text is Edward Franklin Frazier, who was a contributing author to the *Black Church in America*. Franklin states the following in his historical account:

> There was one element in their African heritage that was able to survive capture in Africa and the 'middle passage'—dancing, the most primitive form of religious expression. The slaves were encouraged to dance during the 'middle passage' and in the West Indies the slaves were forced to dance as a part of the breaking-in process. In the

---

[9] Hart Nelson, et al., eds., *The Black Church in America*, (New York: Basic Books, Inc., 1971), 19.

'shout-songs' on the Sea Islands off the coast of South Carolina and Georgia one may discover the remnants of the African religious heritage. However, no African religious cults became established on American soil. The whites did everything possible to suppress these 'heathenish' practices. The Established Church with its emphasis upon a knowledge of the catechism for baptism and with its religious ritual requiring decorum did not make much progress among the slaves. It was only with the coming of the Baptist and Methodist missionaries that the slaves found a form of religion in which they could give expression to their deepest emotions.[10]

In the book, *Black Religion*, Joseph R. Washington begins with a commonly known and held theory and then builds on it to give us a picture of his view of the historical context of the African American church. He states the following:

> The church was the first community or public organization that the Negro actually owned and completely controlled. And it is possibly true to this day that the Negro church is the most thoroughly owned and controlled public institution of the race. Nothing can compare with the ownership and control except ownership of the home and possibly control of the Negro lodge. It is to be doubted whether Negro control is as complete in any other area of Negro life, except these two, as it is in the

---

[10] Frazier, *The Negro Church in America*, 82.

church.[11]

Another historical view and perspective of the beginnings of the African American church come out of the book, *Pastoral Theology: A Black Perspective*. This work approaches the history of the black church from the perspective of showing the injustices of the institutional white church. In this work, Harris asserts the following:

Now, what do white evangelicals mean when they say that Jesus will set you free? What is their understanding of freedom? We believe that they mean essentially that Jesus will free one from the grips of personal sin such as drunkenness, lust, or envy. However, when the black preacher in the tradition of black experiential religion says that Jesus will set you free, he or she is talking about freedom not simply from the catalogue of sins to which white evangelicals and fundamentalists so often refer. The black preacher also means freedom from oppression and injustice.[12]

With this perspective in mind, one can easily see the African American church was born out of a different mindset as it relates to its theological viewpoints.

A work by Roosevelt Robinson, Jr., which was a research paper presented to the Faculty of the Graduate School of

---

[11] Joseph R. Washington, *Black Religion: The Negro and Christianity in the United States*, (Boston: Beacon Press, 1964), 41.

[12] James H. Harris, *Pastoral Theology A Black-Church Perspective*, (Minneapolis: Fortress Press, 1991), 11.

Florida Beacon College, contains a richly detailed history of the *History of the Black Baptist Church*. Robinson chose to write about the struggles and progress of the Black Baptist Church, first of all, because he believed the Black Baptist Church tradition has something positive to offer American Christianity.[13] One cannot read this research paper, which entails only a very small portion of Black Baptist history, without having a greater respect and appreciation for such a people.

Now, attention on the basic history of the most popular denominational groups in the African American community will be viewed. The following groups will receive special attention: National Baptist Convention of America, Inc., National Baptist Convention, U.S.A., Inc., African Methodist Episcopal Church, African Methodist Episcopal Zion Church, and the Church of God In Christ. The history of these churches will be observed as documented in the *Handbook of Denominations in the United States*, by Frank S. Mead.

"National Baptists" has been the name of some aspect of organized black Baptist life since 1886 at the latest.[14] During the three decades following the Civil War, both the longtime free and the recently freed Baptists of African American descent were developing their public life, including organized church life.[15] By 1876 all of the

---

[13] Roosevelt Robinson Jr., *A People Risen Up Out Of Struggle: The History of the Black Baptist Church*, (A research paper presented to the Faculty of the Graduate School of Florida Beacon College, 1981), I.

[14] Frank S. Mead, *Handbook of Denominations in the United States*, (Nashville: Abingdon Press 10th edition, 1995), 68.

[15] Ibid.

Southern states except Florida had a state missionary convention.[16] But smaller bodies had existed since the 1830's in the Midwest, and organized missionary efforts date back to that same period in the North.[17]

These institutional efforts matured in 1895 when the National Baptist Convention, U.S.A., came into being in an Atlanta gathering. For the next twenty years a single National Baptist body functioned through a variety of activities, publishing Sunday school material being a major one. Also, they sponsored foreign mission enterprises, especially to African and Caribbean countries. [18]

Then in 1915, a schism occurred that produced two National conventions. The one being described here, the NBC of America, Inc., was originally known as the NBC, Inc. (incorporated in 1988). The other took NBC, U.S.A., Inc., as its name. The occasion for the separation was conflict over legal ownership of the publishing house. The "of America" segment followed the Boyd party – that is, the leadership of the Reverend R.H. Boyd. The other sector took the side of the Reverend E. C. Morris, who had been National Baptist president since 1897.[19]

The National Baptist Convention, U.S.A., Inc. is the largest body of black Baptists in the U.S., and it shares a common history with the "of America" denomination (just described)

---

[16] Ibid.
[17] Ibid.
[18] Ibid.
[19] Ibid.

throughout the formative years.[20] Its formal origins date from 1895, with many roots and predecessors stretching back to the period around 1840. Until the disagreement that arose over control of the publishing house of the denomination in 1915, there was a single National Baptist body. Once the "of America" convention was created, the Foreign Mission Board became the "U.S.A." body's center of operations.[21]

The African Methodist Episcopal Church, which is one of the three largest Methodist groups in the U.S., began in 1787 when a number of members of St. George's Methodist Episcopal Church in Philadelphia withdrew in protest against racial discrimination.[22] They built Bethel Chapel with the assistance of Bishop William White of the Protestant Episcopal Church. Francis Asbury dedicated the chapel in Philadelphia and ordained Richard Allen as its minister. The body was formally organized as the African Methodist Episcopal Church in 1816; in the same year, Allen was consecrated as its first bishop, again by Bishop Asbury.[23]

The African Methodist Episcopal Zion Church dates from 1796, when it was organized by a group of members protesting discrimination in the John Street Church in New York City.[24] Their first church, named Zion, was built in

---

[20] Ibid., 69.
[21] Ibid.
[22] Ibid.,199.
[23] Ibid.
[24] Ibid., 200.

1800, and that word was later made part of the denominational name. The first annual conference was held in that church in 1821, with 19 preachers from six black Methodist churches in New Haven, Connecticut; Philadelphia, Pennsylvania; and Newark, New Jersey, presided over by the Reverend William Phoebus of the white Methodist Episcopal Church. James Varick, who had led the John Street dissension, was elected the first bishop. The present name was approved in 1848. The church spread quickly over the Northern states, and by 1880 there were 15 annual conferences in the South.[25]

Ministers C. H. Mason and C. P. Jones, rejected by Baptist groups in Arkansas for what was considered an overemphasis on Holiness, founded the Church of God in Christ (Memphis) in 1897. The name was divinely revealed to Mason, who stressed entire sanctification and had received in a revival the baptism of the Holy Spirit, together with "signs of speaking with tongues." Today there are 6,500,000 members in 12,186 churches worldwide, and it is the largest Pentecostal denomination in the world today.[26]

As stated earlier, large bodies of information were not prevalent in the early history of the African American church. This fact should not be strange when one views the circumstances involved in such a history. Considering the situation in which a people who were uprooted from their homeland without consent and brought to an unfamiliar land, preserving the legacy of history was not on their

---

[25] Ibid.
[26] Ibid.,114.

minds. Also, consider that early in the African American experience in America, most African Americans could not read nor write and neither did their masters want to teach them; therefore, they did not have the capacity to preserve nor record the historical data. Finally, when one considers that there was no national organizational structure in place to synthesize what was happening and no network available, then it can be easily understood why historical matters would not be plentiful and why what is available is rather sketchy.

As seen in the beginnings of the African American church in the United States, there are several things that are worthy of one's consideration, which has had a huge impact on the church today. First, the concept of Christianity in the new world was introduced to the African Americans slaves, for the most part, by the African American slave owners and by evangelistically-minded Baptists. Secondly, the African American church was birthed out of the fact that the white Americans, for the most part, discriminated against the African American community especially in the context of their church institutions and worship services. Third, the church became somewhat of a safe haven where the African American people could escape the oppression of their masters. Fourth, in history, the church became a place that the African American people could control and call their own. Fifth, by splits and divisions in the churches more people would rise and become giants or stand-outs in the church world. Sixth, because of heavy restrictions and limitations placed upon African Americans, the church easily became the social center and seat of power for the African American communities as a whole.

This author will now elaborate on the above points. First, the concept of Christianity in the new world was introduced, for the most part, by the African American slave owners and by evangelistically-minded Baptists. Roger Williams founded the first Baptist church on American soil in 1639, and the years following were characterized by continued slow growth. By 1740, there were Baptist Churches in every colony.[27] The Baptist Church is the oldest continuously organized group in America.[28] From the very start, there were two things that stood out about the Baptists: their religious beliefs and their church organization were deeply democratic, and their approach was highly evangelistic.

In the 1740's, with the great revival in America brewing, the Baptist church began to grow even more. Working from an evangelistic conviction, the Baptist church brought the Christian religion to America's African American community. The role of the Baptist Church in Black religious education was so great that, along with the Methodists, they substantially took over the spiritual development of most American Blacks, while the churches that had been active during the earlier period fell far behind.[29]

In as much as the Christian religion was introduced to blacks by whites, it is interesting to note how it was introduced; what was shared and what was kept a secret. It was from the Bible that the slaves learned of the god of the white man and of his ways with the world and with men.[30] The slaves were taught that the God with whom they became

---

[27] Robinson, *A People Risen Up Out of Struggle: The History of the Black Baptist Church*, 4.
[28] Ibid.
[29] Ibid., 5.
[30] Frazier. *The Negro Church in America*, 11.

acquainted in the Bible was the ruler of the universe and superior to all other gods.[31] They were taught that the God of the Bible punished and rewarded black men as well as white men.[32] Black men were expected to accept their lot in this world and if they were obedient and honest and truthful they would be rewarded in the world after death.[33]

Secondly, the African American church was birthed out of the fact that white Americans, for the most part, discriminated against the African American community, especially in the context of their church institutions and worship services.

Because of a common belief held by most whites that blacks were inferior, there was a huge problem in white America accepting African Americans as equal. So, as what we have seen earlier in the history of the African American church, it was uncommon for blacks to have any positions of service or authority in white congregations. This then led to the formation of African American churches that were eventually independent of white control.

Third, the church became somewhat of a safe haven where African American people could escape the oppression of their masters. For the slaves who worked and suffered in an alien world, religion offered a means of catharsis for their pent-up emotions and frustrations.[34] Moreover, it turned

---

[31] Ibid.
[32] Ibid.
[33] Ibid.
[34] Ibid., 45.

their minds from the sufferings and privations of this world to a world after death where the weary would find rest and victims of injustices would be compensated.[35] The church, in essence, served as somewhat of an escape, so long as it offered no threat to the white man's dominance in both economic and social relations.

Fourth, in history, the church became a place that the African American people could control and call their own. Once the churches began to develop they had their own pastors and other officers that they elected. Once the national church took shape, the African Americans had their own Bishops and other officers. This, of course, would mean a lot if you have always been in a world that was completely dominated and controlled by your master. The following statement was made by Kelly Brown Douglas in the *Journal of Religious Thought*:

> The black church is, however, unique as a social institution. As one of the few black institutions to survive slavery, it is the one black social institution that remains virtually free from white control. That observation is particularly true for the black independent church tradition – that is, African Methodist Episcopal (AME), African Methodist Episcopal Zion (AMEZ), National and Progressive Baptist, and so forth.[36]

---

[35] Ibid.

[36] Kelly Brown Douglass and Ronald E Hopson, "Understanding the Black Church: The Dynamics of Change," *In Journal of Religious Thought*. 56/57 (Spring-Fall 2001) [journal on-line]; available from http://search.epnet.com/direct.asp?an=12233630&db=rlh; Internet; accessed 23

Fifth, by splits and divisions in the churches more people would rise and become giants or stand-outs in the African American church world. As churches during slavery time and shortly thereafter began to emerge, people flocked to these sanctuaries. As the churches came into existence they required leadership. As more churches, organizations, and ministries developed, they required even more leadership. Also, with this in mind, if there were large numbers of people in one church and only one leader then others could rise to prominence if there was a split or an unresolved issue. If another church started, it would also give more people a chance at leadership. Given the culture of slavery, the church was the only place where some African American men could be in charge and have some authority.

Finally, because of heavy restrictions and limitations placed upon African Americans, the church easily became the social center and seat of power for the African American communities as a whole. Large numbers of African Americans were never permitted to gather in one place for fear of some kind of uprising. Where they were permitted to gather was at church, as long as it was peaceful and it appeared to pose no threat to the white man. Because of this unique situation, everything that needed to be communicated to the masses of people was generally done at church. If there was some news of importance, good or bad, it was communicated at church. It can easily be seen in this scenario that the church became an important institution in the African American community.

March 2005.

This first chapter concerning a brief study of the history of the African American Church will serve as a basis from which we will begin to look for unique challenges faced by the African American pastors in the South. This history will impact not only African American pastors in the South, but churches and pastors in America of all races, sizes, and geographical locations.

CHAPTER 2

THEOLOGICAL AND THEORETICAL VIEWPOINTS

In this chapter, the discussion centers on the theological rationale for the study, the theoretical rationale behind the study, and finally a review of the current information available on the subject of the African American pastor in the South. Considerable attention will be given to the theoretical rationale behind the study, in as much as this strikes at the core of the motivation for this author. Also, as the study is made of the current information available on the subject of the African American pastor in the South, the information viewed will be general and not just limited to the South. Finally, this author hopes to contribute to the general body of knowledge the unique challenges faced by African American pastors in the South.

As a study of the theological rationale is made, this author is aware the Bible does not directly address a black church or a white church; a big church or a small church; a church in the North and or a church in the South. The Bible does, however, address the church universally, as the body of Christ, and the church local, as a group of believers in a certain location, such as the church at Corinth, Ephesus, or Rome. So, the theological rationale for the unique challenges of African American pastors of small churches in the South is one of considering the principles needed to be effective at ministering to the African American culture. First, there must be a consideration of the homogeneous principle that is at work with all people groups. According to the homogeneous principle, people like to become Christians "without having to cross racial, linguistic, or class barriers to do so."[37] In his book, *Shepherding the Small Church*, Glenn Daman highlights this issue. He states, "Every sociological group has a distinct set of cultural norms and expectations that set it apart from other groups. The church is no different. People associate with one another because they have certain similarities and bonds that connect them with shared expectations, ideals, norms, values, and behavior patterns."[38]

In light of the above premise, the basic theological rationale for such a study is the Bible declaration in Proverbs 4:7: "Wisdom is the principle thing, therefore get wisdom: and with all thy getting get an understanding." Being aware of the traditions, cultures, challenges, and customs of the people who were being ministered to, ensured that the ministry of Jesus, Paul, Peter, and other New Testament personalities were more effective. For example, Paul circumcised Timothy, even though circumcision was not a requirement for membership in the Church. Acts 16:3 states, "Him would Paul have to go forth with him; and took and circumcised him because of the Jews which were in those quarters: for they knew all that his father was a Greek." Paul made an adjustment in his view of

---

[37] Peter C. Wagner, *Church Growth State of the Art*, (Wheaton: Tyndale House, 1986), 291.

[38] Glenn Daman, *Shepherding the Small Church*, (Grand Rapids, MI: Published by Kregal Publications, a division of Kregal, Inc., 2002), 42.

circumcision in order to be more effective to the people of that region. This occurred because Paul had knowledge of the people to whom he was ministering. In the same way, it is this author's belief that if one has specific knowledge of the people being served and governs himself accordingly, ministry will be more effective, because there will be a clear focus and because there will be an awareness of the hurdles that must be overcome.

> Furthermore, Paul states in I Corinthians 9:19-23, "For though I be free from all men, yet have I made myself servant unto all, that I might gain the more. And unto the Jews I became as a Jew, that I might gain the Jews; to them that are under the law, as under the law, that I might gain them that are under the law; To them that are without law, as without law, (being not without law to God, but under the law to Christ,) that I might gain them that are without law. To the weak became I as weak, that I might gain the weak: I am made all things to all men, that I might by all means save some. And this I do for the gospel's sake, that I might be partaker thereof with you."

In the teaching of this passage, Paul outlines the ultimate goal as winning men to Christ, and he states that whatever sacrifice is necessary, it must be done. So, when one has winning men to Christ as his aim and priority, there will be an infiltration among all people groups in all locations. Thus, considerations and adjustments will be made, having one measurement of success: Are people being won to Christ?

As it pertains to the move from the theological to the theoretical, this author's theoretical presuppositions are many, and they are as follows:

First, this author believes there are distinct differences and challenges that are faced by the African American pastors of small churches in the South. This belief is based on personal experience and observation, the history of the African American church in the South which was discussed in the previous chapter, conversations with those of different ethnic groups, surveys conducted by this author, which will be viewed in the next chapter, and by research of the current literature which will be acknowledged later in the current chapter.

The second theoretical presupposition is that often these unique challenges are neither considered nor factored into the equation when those outside the African American community are giving non-Biblical information as it relates to church growth, church operations, general church information, church surveys, etc. As an example, this author attended a national conference targeted at small churches in small counties in America. There was great information given and great discussions surrounding the state of small churches and pastors of these small churches. However, on the Board of this host organization, there were no African Americans represented, there were no African Americans on the rostrum to speak at this national conference, and there was only one African American Pastor registered to attend; this author was the only African American registered. Some questions that are raised in this pastor's mind are:

    (1) Why were there no other African Americans represented?

    (2) Was the tone of the conference not inviting to African Americans?

    (3) What will it take to bring African American pastors to

such a conference?

(4) Are non-African American pastors willing to do what it will take to be inclusive? In fairness to this particular conference, it was accessible to anyone who wanted to attend, and this author was treated with respect and dignity.[39]

In a book entitled, *Congregations in America*, by Mark Chaves, a total of 1,236 churches were surveyed. In this survey, only 8% of the people surveyed were in the South and only 11.9% of those congregations in the South was led by an African American pastor.[40] These numbers indicate that when one is viewing sources such as this to get a picture of what congregation life is like in America, for the most part, they are not good indicators of what congregation life is like in the African American churches. In fairness to the book, *Congregations in America*, by Mark Chaves, the author states, "There is, however, a straightforward reason why sampling congregations lagged behind sampling other types of organizations: there is no adequate sampling frame -no comprehensive list of American congregations - from which to select randomly a nationally representative sample of congregations."[41] If this is true for the church world in general, it is an even greater truth in the African American community.

In the book, *The Black Church in the African American*

---

[39] Jim Graff, *Significant Church Conference*, Victoria, TX, 13-15 November 2006.
[40] Mark Chaves, *Congregations In America*, (Cambridge, Massachusetts: Harvard University Press, 2004), 226.
[41] Ibid., 213.

Experience, which is the latest major research that this author was able to find, the following observation was reported.

> "Current scholarship on black churches is plagued by a lack of reliable statistical data. For example, since surveys are lacking, no one knows the accurate membership figures for most black denominations. There is also a paucity of other kinds of data on the finances of the black churches; the education, income, and occupational status of black clergy; and the kinds of groups and programs which support the churches' internal life and community outreach. The last major field study of both urban and rural black churches covering these kinds of information was done by Benjamin Mays and Joseph Nicholson in 1933, almost sixty years ago. Their study covered 609 urban churches and 185 rural churches."[42]

Finally, another example to show that African American Pastors are not adequately represented in books, conferences, studies, etc. is found in the book, *God's Potters: Pastoral Leadership and the Shaping of Congregations*, by Jackson W. Carroll. In this landmark study, the author addresses what life is like in congregations in America and, in particular, the life of the pastor. The author bases the study, to a large extent, on 832 respondents of a survey. In one of a number of surveys conducted, 81% were white pastors and only 15% where

---

[42] C. Eric Lincoln and Lawrence H. Mamiya, *The Black Church in the African American Experience*, (Durham: Duke University Press, 1990), 93.

African American pastors.[43]

The third theoretical presupposition is there is very minimal information available on the unique challenges of the African American pastors of small churches in the South; this is in spite of the very pronounced movement to deal with the smaller congregations that have emerged in the last thirty years. Even with the attention that has been given to small churches in general, there is still limited written information that highlights the smaller churches pastored by African Americans in the South. Again, it is the hope of this author's study to add to and address this deficiency in these writings.

The fourth theoretical presupposition is this author strongly believes the way the African American church was birthed in America has a great deal to do with its present-day challenges and obstacles. Factors such as a lack of clergy education, less than average economic resources, a crisis of identity, broad clergy accountability problems, deep-seated unscriptural traditions, etc., are all worthy of consideration when attempting to discover why there are unique challenges of our targeted study group. One such example of an obstacle is highlighted in the book, *The Church in the Life of the Black Family,* by Wallace Charles Smith. He states the following in describing some early facts of origin in America:

> "Unfortunately, however, the Bible was also taught by unscrupulous slave masters as the authoritative

---

[43] Jackson W. Carroll, *God's Potters: Pastoral Leadership and the Shaping of Congregations,* (Grand Rapids, MI.: William B. Eerdmans Publishing Company, 2006), 275.

source for obedience to one's master and acceptance of one's curse, which was marked by one's blackness. For the black church to model the freeing power which is necessary to liberate persons from the negative myths that have been perpetrated upon its people, the Bible must be allowed to speak for itself and eisegesis such as that which produces the ludicrous interpretations of Ham's curse must be vehemently denied and replaced by a hermeneutic which lets God speak." [44]

These ideas must be overcome inside and outside of the African American community. It is sad living in the South in 2007 and still coming in contact with this kind of teaching that is perpetrated by some of our brothers and sisters.

The fifth theoretical presupposition is that this author contends there are some positives as well as negatives as it relates to the origin of the African American church in a general sense; in particular, in the deep rural South. Some of those positives could be a strong sense of loyalty, a strong commitment to family, and a good spiritual heritage. This is because the church was all that some African Americans had in the early years. With this in mind, the African American church was and still is the only major institution that is owned and exclusively run by African Americans in their communities. One of the negatives would be the educational and economic barriers that must be overcome. The African American community would be

---

[44] Charles Wallace Smith, *The Church in the Life of the Black Family*, (Valley Forge, PA.: Judson Press, 1993), 48.

and still is playing catch up in comparison to the white community.

Furthermore, the theoretical presupposition is also inherent in the general notion or attitude that those who live in urban areas in the North are "better off" than those who live in the South. This point is amplified by the following statement from D. E. Lindstrom in his book, *American Rural Life*: "People living in rural communities should realize that most of them will live there all of their lives and that they should do something to make the community a better place in which to live. To do so they need to be led to look at themselves critically. Then, recognizing their shortcomings, they should be helped to build up their business, religious, educational, health, social, and recreational life to the level enjoyed by urban people."[45]

Finally, an interesting presupposition flows out of the research report completed by Duke's Pulpit & Pew, an interdenominational project. The report states, "African Americans who fled the rural South in droves during the first half of the twentieth century left many small, struggling rural churches and spawned a host of urban congregations in the cities where they moved. In the 1970s, however, a gradual reverse migration began as both older and college-educated blacks moved back to the South, attracted by improved race relations, economic prospects, and cultural and family ties. These trends have created a positive context for black churches in the South, but they also pose

---

[45] David Edgar Lindstrom, *American Rural Life*, (New York: The Ronald Press Company, 1948), 376.

new challenges to churches as increasingly well-educated constituents demand an educated black clergy."[46] In essence, it is this author's opinion that the African American church in the South is changing, and it is because of the African Americans with wealth and education who are coming back to the South and unconsciously forcing the change.

---

[46] Lawrence Mamiya, *River of Struggle, River of Freedom: Trends in Black Churches and Black Pastoral Leadership*, Research Report from Pulpit & Pew, Research on Pastoral Leadership, (Durham, N`.C.: Duke Divinity School, 2005).

CHAPTER 3

LITERARY REVIEW

As this author has probed and attempted to research the available literature on the subject of the unique challenges faced by African American Pastors of small churches in the South, a few observations are warranted. The first observation: there is a definite shortage of available information. It must be also noted that the limited available information is very insightful. Secondly, a great portion of the information which is available comes from popular sources as opposed to scholarly sources; therefore the credibility of the information is often questionable. Finally, most of the literature does not single out the Deep South, except for some isolated incidences. Therefore, a lot of information that one gathers must be skimmed from the general pool of knowledge related to pastors and churches as a whole.

In respect to the literary review on this subject matter, this author will divide the review into three categories. The first category will be information from authors outside the African American community and their writings about the smaller church, the church in the South and pastoring a smaller church. Such literature as *Southern Churches in Crises*, *Smaller Churches Healthy and Growing*, *The Journal of a Southern Pastor*, and *Shepherding the Smaller Church* will be critiqued. The second category will focus on literature compiled by African American scholars and pastors. Some of the material for review will be *Fortress Introduction to Black Church History, Black Church Beginnings, The Black Church in the Post-Civil Rights Era, The Church in the Life of the Black Family, Church Planting in the African American Context, Church Growth from an African American Perspective*, etc. The third category will consist of research works such as *Congregations in America, God's Potters: Pastoral Leadership and the Shaping of Congregations*, and *The Black Church in the African American Experience*.

Professor Samuel S. Hill, Jr. in his book, *Southern Churches in Crisis*, spoke to the changes which were occurring in the South in the early 1960's. The reason this author is struck by these writings, despite the age of the book, is that some of the issues today had its foundation in the distant history of the South. In his book Hill addresses the social changes in the South and how the Church in the South was coping with the issue of social change. This author is struck by Hill's honesty as it relates to writing the book. Hill's talk of the church is limited to the "white church," and he makes the following statement in his introduction:

> The book is inevitably unbalanced because of one monumental omission: Negro Protestantism in the South is nowhere treated in depth. Grievous - or inexcusable- as this omission may seem, it is consistent with the religious state of things in Dixie. Although it would appear that "popular southern religion" includes the faith-life of southern Negroes - especially since a huge majority of them belong to the same two denominations that dominate the white culture - this is simply not the case. Negro and white religion are different, resisting meaningful comparison under the same categories. Competence in dealing with the religion of the white society does not ensure facility in treating what Joseph Washington calls "black religion." The definitive work on the southern Negro church has

not been written, and one suspects that only a southern Negro could produce it. [47]

This author agrees with Hill that the work of the African American church can best be properly understood and written by an African American.

Also in Hill's book, another interesting comment lets the world in on some thought processes of the way some white Americans in the South were thinking in the day in which the book was written. Even though some things have changed, there are yet some things that remain the same. In the chapter dealing with the threat of rejection, we find the following comment. "Several factors work against the church's remaining a significant factor in Negro life: The record of the white church in using religion as a means of keeping Negroes docile and oriented to life in the next world; The record of the Negro church in reducing faith to mere emotion; And the Negro church's obsequious dealings with the (white) community power structure. If these recollections stand out, the church will have become obsolescent for the new Negro. Also, wherever material and political deprivations sear the Negro's spirit, and Christianity is confined to otherworldly concerns, the church will be spurned."[48] It is also interesting to note that Hill writes in a manner that suggests two different churches in the South, one black, and one white. Although this may not be the prevailing view that would be in print today, there are yet seeds of this thought process still alive and the

---

[47] Samuel S. Hill Jr. *Southern Churches in Crisis*, (Chicago: Holt, Rinehart and Winston, 1966, 1967), xvi.
[48] Ibid., 190.

residue of the former thoughts are still detected, even today in the Deep South.

In a random bookstore visit in Columbus, GA. this author decided to purchase some books on small churches in an attempt to become informed on the literature available concerning this subject. After viewing the shelves, two books were retrieved, one entitled *Smaller Churches Healthy and Growing* by Barry Campbell and another entitled *Shepherding the Small Church* by Glenn Daman. As we continue to look at some books written by those outside the African American community, this experience underscores a particular thought process, which is that most of the material written by non-African Americans doesn't include African Americans. As an example in both these two books, there is no reference to an African American pastor or church in the examples. In the book on *Smaller Churches Healthy and Growing*, Barry Campbell highlights six churches as models of healthy and growing churches; all of them are Baptists and all are non-African American. Although, there is one reference made to African Americans attending a church, the church is Gardena-Torrence Southern Baptist Church located in Los Angeles, California. "Gardena-Torrance is located in a multiracial, multiethnic community. The congregation includes Anglos, Hawaiians, and African – Americans."[49] When an African American pastor views the examples of healthy churches he is not included. When the principles to be a healthy church are discussed, such as evangelism, discipleship, fellowship, ministry, and worship, all churches can relate. Finally, when

---

[49] Barry Campbell, *Smaller Churches Healthy and Growing*, (Nashville, TN: Lifeway Press, 1998), 23.

the illustrations and practical part are discussed there is some cultural divides that are noticeable.

The book by Glenn Daman entitled *Shepherding the Small Church* states the following:

To be effective we must first understand the people we are called to serve. Without such an understanding we will develop programs that fail to reach the people we have targeted to serve. Understanding community involves more than just being familiar with the names and faces of people. To penetrate the subculture of the community and to reach people requires an in-depth understanding of the mindset and thinking of people. We need to know who people are and what they like. We need to understand their needs, their hurts, their struggles, their pressures, and their desires. Attempting to build an effective church without knowledge of the community is like trying to build a boat without understanding the waters it will ply. A boat built for inland waterways will be far different from one made to sail the ocean. A ship designed for Arctic exploration will be constructed differently than a cruise ship. It is not enough to know how to build boats; we must know the intended purpose of the boat. [50]

In like manner, the different churches are all boats, but it appears that the African American church is, for the time being, plying in different waters.

The last document viewed is from authors outside the African American community, which is a Journal entitled,

---

[50] Glenn Daman, *Shepherding the Small Church*, 22.

The Journal of a Southern Pastor written by Joseph B. Gremillion. This is another older document with the setting in the 1950's; although it is from the previous generation it helps us to understand some of the pain of this generation and it explains the residue of some negative attitudes and actions that we have in this present generation. In his journal, Joseph B. Gremillion, who was a Catholic priest over a parish in Shreveport, LA., talks about some of the social issues that he fought against in his own parish. In this dissertation an excerpt from his journal is included to demonstrate an inner look at some of the race issues in the South; it is important to emphasize that this writing is from a white American talking about the conversation and exchange of other whites. This conversation takes place after Gremillion had attempted to hold an interracial meeting in the cafeteria of the church.[51]

Four men are on the steps of the church and Gremillion is walking by:

> "You're pushing this nigger business too far, Father. It's all right to give the nigger better wages and more schooling, but this business of social equality, no sir! You're from the South, too, aren't you? You know we've gotta keep segregation and we're GONNA keep segregation."
>
> "Yes, I'm from the South, south Louisiana on top of it. Born and reared on a cotton and cane farm down there. My dad had Negro share-croppers – maybe

---

[51] J.B. Gremillion, *A Journal of a Southern Pastor*, (Chicago: Fides Publishers Association, 1957), 44.

that's what opened my eyes. My granddad fought in the Confederate Army. I remember when my grandmother's personal slave servant died. Yes, I'm from the South and I've a lot to make up for."

"Well, Father, what are you aiming at? Why did you invite those colored folks for a meeting here? Are you trying to break down the wall of segregation?"

"Sure, I'm trying to destroy segregation."
"You don't mean you're for social equality, too!"

"Sure, I am. I frequently have Negro friends in for dinner at the Rectory."[52]

This writing, although it may be uncomfortable for some people today or even embarrassing, it is yet recorded as a part of history. This author includes this exchange to suggest that out of this kind of climate comes a unique challenge faced by African American pastors in the South. This one challenge which will be discussed later concerns attitudes and hurts on the part of whites and blacks.

The Journal of a Southern Pastor also highlights that all attitudes were not and are not negative in the South. In the midst of this time, Father Gremillion was involved in trying to correct the problem of racism in the South. He gave a powerful speech to the Annual Teachers' Institute of the Diocese of Lafayette. This speech came in response to an incidence of violence perpetrated against an African

---

[52] Ibid., 44-45.

American child.[53] The speech was given to specifically address the issues of race. Father Gremillion gave four reasons why the Negro should be accepted. The four reasons outlined in his speech are: (1) we must receive the Negro, on a status fully equal and without reserve, into our Church and school and society for the advance of the world-wide mission of Christ. (2) We must strive toward receiving the Negro on a status fully equal and without reserve into our Church and school and society because to deny the Negro such status is to be guilty of the heresy of racism. (3) We must receive our Negro Catholics into the full life of the Church and society because they are members of the Mystical Body of Christ. (4) We must receive the Negro into the full life of the Church and society because this is the way of Christian perfection.[54]

The second section of the review of literature involves those scholars and authors who are a part of the African American community and involves their writings and perspective. The first book viewed is *Fortress Introduction to Black Church History* by Anne H. Pinn and Anthony B. Pinn. Anne H. Pinn is Pastor of Mt. Zion A.M.E. Church, Buffalo, New York, and President of the African Methodist Ministers' Alliance. She is also the mother of Anthony B. Pinn. Their concise writings are an overview of the history of major black religious bodies: namely Methodist, Baptist, and Pentecostal. Secondly, these authors are concerned with the black church and social justice.

The authors, Pinn and Pinn, acquaint their readers with two

---

[53] Ibid., 269.
[54] Ibid., 276-281.

schools of thought that shape some of the preaching and theology of African Americans in general. The social gospel is given definition by these authors in the chapter "Liberation Thought and the Black Church." The authors state, "A potent approach to social transformation within churches during the 1800s and the early 1900s was the social gospel (or social Christianity as it is commonly called). This activist interpretation of the Gospel of Christ first hit print and church agendas when those such as Walter Rauschenbusch urged Christians to apply their faith to the elevation of poverty."[55] In other words, the social gospel is a suggestion that Jesus Christ is concerned about the total man; spirit, soul, body. Pinn and Pinn further explain that:

> Religious leaders and theologians like Rauschenbusch recognized that the industrialization of the twentieth century was at best a mixed blessing in that it promoted wealth and stability, but only a small percentage of the population actually benefited from capitalism's economic boom. In essence, the cliché is correct, the "rich got richer and the poor got poorer." Although beneficial on the surface, this version for the social gospel often held a deep-seated racial chauvinism. In other words, for some social gospelers the movement of the Christians in the social realm was justified by a racist sense of manifest destiny by which white Christians in the United States were recognized as God's chosen people, divinely selected to dominate the earth.[56]

---

[55] Anne H. Pinn and Anthony B. Pinn, *Fortress To Black Church History*, (Minneapolis: Fortress Press, 2002), 127.
[56] Ibid.

Some of the names associated with the social gospel are Fannie Lou Hamer, James Walker Hood, Martin Luther King Jr., Adam Clayton Powell Jr., and Ida B. Wells-Barnett.

In addition to the social gospel, this book also informs the reader of black liberation theology. One definition of black theology which was given by Pinn and Pinn in their book is:

> Black Theology is a theology of black liberation. It seeks to plumb the black condition in the light of God's revelation in Jesus Christ, so that the black community can see that the gospel is commensurate with the achievement of black humanity. Black Theology is a theology of "blackness." It is the affirmation of black humanity that emancipates black people from white racism, thus providing authentic freedom for both white and black people. It affirms the humanity of white people in that it says No to the encroachment of white oppression.[57]

In light of the history of the African American plight, it is easy to see how in a people's experience will flow their interpretation, or interpretation can be based on experience. The Bible says in Luke 4:18-19, "The Spirit of the Lord is upon me, because he hath anointed me to preach the gospel to the poor; he hath sent me to heal the brokenhearted, to preach deliverance to the captives, and recovering of sight to the blind, to set at liberty them that bruised, To preach the acceptable year of the Lord." If an oppressed people read such a passage the belief could

---

[57] Ibid., 159.

easily emerge that Jesus Christ wants to liberate any person who is bound by oppression and especially slavery and its effects. Some of the names attached to black theology are Jaramogi Abebe Agyeman, James Hal Cone, Pauli Murray, J. Deotis Roberts, and Gayraud S. Wilmore Jr.

The next book in this second section of the review of the literature, which is authored by an African American, is *The Black Church in the Post-Civil Rights Era*, written by Anthony B. Pinn. In this work, Pinn concerns himself with the historical and theological background of the African American church and then certain themes in contemporary customs or practices. In the historical background, such things as the church and its relationship to Africa, the great migration and religious diversification, the church and the civil rights movement, and the Black church in decline are discussed. As pertaining to the theological background, Pinn discusses what the African American church believes and worships as a celebration of belief. Themes in contemporary praxis focus on the black church on economic issues, the black church on health and sexuality, and sexism and church ministry.

Of particular interest to this present author is the discussion of the great migration from the South to the North after the Civil War period. This migration will serve to set the stage for the differences seen in the African American churches of the North as opposed to the South. Pinn observes:

> Black denominations in existence near the close of the nineteenth century were forever changed by what is commonly called the Great Migration, beginning during the late years of the nineteenth century and continuing through the first three decades of the twentieth century. To give some sense of the numbers involved, by 1920 roughly 500,000 black Americans moved to the North, and by 1930 more than 1.5 million had moved out of the South. Whites, afraid of the potential economic

and social ramifications of this mass movement, attempted to coerce black Americans into remaining in the South. Yet, in spite of the often hostile-legal and extralegal-white resistance and some reluctance on the part of black leaders such as Frederick Douglass and numerous black church leaders, the motivation for moving was far too great.[58]

Another point of interest in Pinn's writings is the discussion of how the black church was closely aligned with the black community and the social issues of that era. He states that this blending of social protest and Christian faith resulted in many scholars, preachers, and laypeople thinking of the Black Church and black communities as intimately connected. This point to an important and historical intertwining of the Black Church's development and the needs of black Americans, which probably hit its twentieth-century high point with the civil rights movement.[59]

In the post-civil rights era it appears now that the gap between the black community and the black church is growing even wider, which is a unique challenge that the African American pastor has, particularly in the South: how do you get and keep people in church who are living in the shadow of a church that was so tied to the problems of the community?

The final point in Pinn's writings is a discussion on the

---

[58] Anthony B. Pinn, *The Black Church in the Post-Civil Rights Era*, (Maryknoll, New York: Orbis Books, 2002), 7.
[59] Ibid., 18.

present day impact of the mega-church phenomenon. As of 1991, an estimated forty-five churches in the United States had five thousand or more worshipers on a given Sunday. Now there are more than four hundred such churches, thirty-five of which are black churches.[60] Pinn's claim is that whether an active participant or not, black churches in the twenty-first century will have no choice but to think about their ministries and audience in terms of the mega-church phenomenon and its interpretation of the gospel.[61] Some thoughts on the megachurch will be discussed later in this dissertation.

Another book in the second section of the review of literature, which is authored by an African American, is *Black Church Beginnings* by Henry H. Mitchell. As noted on the back cover of this book, Henry H. Mitchell is retired from a wide-ranging academic career as a professor of history, black church studies, and homiletics, most recently at the Interdenominational Theological Center, Atlanta, Georgia.

There are several distinctions about Mitchell's work which are noteworthy for this author's research. One is the claim that Christianity was not exclusively given to the African American people by slave masters. Secondly, in chapter four, Mitchell lays out trends impacting the early black churches up to the 1900's, some of which are still in place today. Finally, the whole of chapter eight deals with the new roles faced by churches and schools during and after the period of reconstruction.

---

[60] Ibid., 135.
[61] Ibid., 139.

First, as to the claim that Christianity was not exclusively given to the African American people by slave masters, there is very little writing concerning this subject. When one views those who did address such matters, there is controversy surrounding the truth of this statement. Nonetheless, Mitchell states, It is my high expectation that those who hold that black religion was given to African Americans by slave masters will be disabused of this dangerous misreading of the facts of the early religious life of the slaves. With this correction, African Americans can be helped to overcome the cripplingly low view of themselves that has been fed not only by errors of history but by subtle messages from the majority culture even today.[62]

Secondly, in chapter four, Mitchell lays out trends impacting the early black churches up to the 1900's, some of which are still in place today. Some of the trends discussed in this work are: caste and class inside the African American churches, North and South; language skills and literacy in a congregation's worship and internal power structures; the roles of laity in the initiation of the proliferation of small churches, as compared to larger urban churches; the placement or distribution of the ministers of various levels of skill and preparation; and the treatment accorded women."[63]

Some examples of the above trends are interesting to observe. As pertaining to class and caste, during the immediate period after slavery, there were some African

---

[62] Henry H. Mitchell, *Black Church Beginnings*, (Grand Rapids: William B. Eerdmans Publishing Company, 2004), xi.
[63] Ibid., 71.

Americans who could read and some who could not. Mitchell observes, "Another necessary functional distinction had to do with basic fluency in English and the simple ability to read the Bible. Leadership in worship made it mandatory that at least one member, preferably the preacher, be able to read."[64] Furthermore, the historic development of whole denominations and of many great churches must be understood to have been conceived and executed by a generation of leaders almost all of whom had been legally and forcibly denied the privilege of learning to read.[65] Another interesting trend mentioned by Mitchell is embodied in the following, "Most of the early history involved other pastors, who served a circuit of churches and traveled by horseback. The size and support of these small churches did not attract the small supply of genuinely talented clergy, so the fact that these churches survived is in large measure attributable to the loyalty and dire need of the laity."[66] The impact of this trend is that still today, the majority of the more educated ministers are in larger churches, and the majority of untrained ministers are in smaller churches.

Finally, the whole of chapter eight deals with the new roles faced by churches and schools during and after the period of reconstruction. After the South was opened up to missionaries, under the protection of military occupation, the Protestant churches of the North launched a veritable crusade to bring literacy to the huge host of the newly

---

[64] Ibid., 72.
[65] Ibid., 73.
[66] Ibid., 77.

freed.[67] The number of African Americans set free in the South is generally accepted to be well over four million. On the face of it, this would seem an impossible total of people to integrate into a working society or functioning communities. This would appear especially true since so many were illiterate and unskilled. After five years of concentrated efforts at instruction, the illiteracy rate had only been reduced to 79.9 % in 1870.[68] As late as the 1890 census, 90 % of African Americans lived in the South, and 80% of those who lived in the South were living in rural areas.[69] This fact of demographics would explain the great difficulties hampering the teaching of needed skills and the forming of needed organizations. This trend is relevant as it relates to the fact that still today there is a high rate of illiteracy in the African American community and also a high rate of churches in rural areas. So the challenge still remains of bringing quality education as it relates to the Word of God to pastors and congregations in the Deep South.

The fourth writing is by Wallace Charles Smith, the author of *The Church in the Life of the Black Family*. Smith's experience has been that of a Pastor; he has served as Professor of the Practice of Ministry at Vanderbilt University Divinity School, Nashville, Tennessee, and was the first African American to serve as a full-time faculty member at Eastern Baptist Seminary in Philadelphia, Pennsylvania. Smith states the following in his introduction:

---

[67] Ibid., 142.
[68] Carter G. Woodson and Charles H. Wesley, *The Negro in Our History*, (Washington, D.C.: Associated Publishers, 1962, 1966), 382.
[69] Lincoln and Mamiya, *The Black Church in the African American Experience*, 95.

"This is a book on pastoral theology. It is also a book on family theology. It is designed as a resource for both pastors and lay leaders in churches that are working on ministries with families. This book is based on the generalization that the black church and the black family have the same roots and similar expressions."[70] The last statement is very opinionated; it may have been true for the first half of the twentieth century but most authors who write about the African American tradition today (2007) would beg to differ with this authors assessment.

Smith also writes about the relationship that exists between the Pastor and the church in the African American experience. His view will shed light on why it would seem that the African American pastor is viewed a little differently than the white pastor. In chapter five, when Smith talks about moving toward a family ministry, he states the following:

> The black church in America retains its vitality against extraordinary odds because it was born as an expression of the black extended family. The ancient tribal structure of Africa was used and improved upon. The consanguineal family models of western Africa were drawn on for inspiration. The black church is an extended family. The pastor functions as chief and male parent. The first lady (or if the pastor is single, a senior mother of the church) functions as female parent. The governing board of deacons, elders, or presbyters functions as the older adults in the consanguineal unit, and the

---

[70]Smith, *The Church in the Life of the Black Family*, 13.

membership at large functions as the siblings.[71]

The next book, written by an African American author, is *Church Growth from an African American Perspective*, by Donald Hilliard Jr. The senior pastor of Cathedral International in Perth Amboy, New Jersey, Donald Hilliard Jr., writes in a very practical manner concerning church growth. In part one Hilliard concerns himself with the fundamentals for a growing church; he talks about understanding church growth, preparing for growth, foundations for healthy church growth, and principles of healthy church growth. In part two of Hilliard's work, he deals with the practical dimensions of purposeful prayer, prophetic preaching, powerful worship, and pertinent ministry.

It is interesting that Hilliard's book is like most other books on church growth with the exception that he writes from an African American perspective, which means that other African Americans will be able to more readily relate to the examples and the paradigm of his approach. One such example of this is found at the beginning of chapter six which is about prophetic preaching. Hilliard says, "A growing African American church is a Bible-preaching and Bible-teaching church with a balanced message between priestly and prophetic ministry. Every ministry and activity of the church centers on the proclamation of the Bible as the true and living Word of God. Although there are many ways for a church to proclaim God's Word, preaching is primary."[72] This would seem true of all growing churches,

---

[71] Ibid., 74.

[72] Donald Hilliard Jr., *Church Growth from an African American*

not just African American churches. So it appears that church growth from an African American perspective is simply that an African American is the author and he is writing from his own personal, cultural perspective.

The final book written by an African American author is *Church Planting in the African American Context* by Hozell C. Francis. Hozell C. Francis, D.Min., is pastor of New Vision Community Church in Inglewood, California. This book definitely digs deep into the African American context at all levels. Such topics as, why African American churches are different than Anglo churches, sociological perspectives of the African American churches, economic factors in African American churches, the hostility factor in the African American community, the homogeneous principle in African American churches, etc. are discussed in detail.

Francis's writings are at the heart of this author's research except that it does not just involve churches and pastors from the South. In spite of this limitation, there is some powerful information that can be gleaned from Francis's work. One such observation is found in chapter six which deals with contemporary preaching in the African American churches; Francis says:

> To best appreciate the experiences and needs of a people, one should have experiences similar to theirs. The tradition of black preaching developed in a context of dire circumstances. The need to engender a degree of hope in a climate of despair led to a particular kind of preaching. In addition, the

---

Perspective, (Vallage Forge, Pennsylvania: Judson Press, 2006), 66.

cultural considerations of African people must be understood. This can be seen in their ecstasy in worship and in their oral tradition. Therefore differences must be seen not in terms of value judgments, but rather as cultural differences first. Only when a matter clearly goes against Scripture can we properly make negative value judgments.[73]

The third section of literature examined concerns some research information in book form concerning churches and pastors. The first one is *Congregations in America* compiled by Mark Chaves, professor of sociology at the University of Arizona and the author of several other books. His work is one of the latest major research projects conducted which draws extensively from the 1998 *National Congregations Study*.

The concern for this present author in the book entitled, *Congregations in America* by Mark Chaves, in which a total of 1,236 churches were surveyed, is the representation of the South and the low number of African Americans included in the survey. In this survey, only 8% of the people surveyed were in the South and only 11.9% of those congregations in the South was led by an African American pastor.[74] These numbers indicate that when one is viewing sources such as this to get a picture of what congregation life is like in America, for the most part; they are not good indicators of what congregation life is like in the African American churches.

---

[73] Hozell C. Francis, *Church Planting in the African American Context*, (Grand Rapids: Zondervan Publishing House, 1999), 62.

[74] Mark Chaves, *Congregations In America*, (Cambridge: Harvard University Press, 2004), 226.

A second work in the area of research conducted on churches and pastors comes from the book, *God's Potters: Pastoral Leadership and the Shaping of Congregations*, by Jackson W. Carroll, who is an ordained United Methodist minister and the retired director of Pulpit and Pew: Research on Pastoral Leadership. In this landmark study, the author addresses what life is like in congregations in America and, in particular, the life of the pastor. The author bases the study, to a large extent, on 832 respondents of a survey. In one of a number of surveys conducted, 81% were white pastors and only 15% were African American pastors.[75] This information is provided to further suggest the challenge in gathering information concerning African American pastors and their unique challenges in the South. As with other studies viewed, this author wants to be clear in communicating that the research and findings are valuable, good, and helpful, but that they may not be a good indicator of the African American community.

In the book *God's Potters: Pastoral Leadership and the Shaping of Congregations*, which is a recent work (2006), the author gives insight into the challenges and changes of Pastors in general. The book talks about Pastoral Leadership at the beginning of the 21st Century. It talks about the social and cultural context in which clergy work. It answers the question: who are God's potters today? The book asks what clergy do and how pastors lead. There is discussion surrounding the major problems of clergy: the problems noted were commitment, satisfaction, and health.
The last book in the research section and the last book

---

[75] Jackson W. Carroll, *God's Potters: Pastoral Leadership and the Shaping of Congregations*, 275.

viewed in this literary review is perhaps the most helpful to the author of this book. The book is entitled, *The Black Church in the African American Experience* by C. Eric Lincoln and Lawrence H. Mamiya. C. Eric Lincoln is Professor of Religion and Culture at Duke University and is the author of numerous books. Lawrence H. Mamiya is Professor of Religion and African Studies at Vassar College.

This milestone research is closely aligned with the suspicions and research of this current author concerning the unique challenges of African American pastors of small churches in the South. One such handicap of this author in doing such a research project is a lack of data. The authors of this book are in agreement with this current author. They suggest, as was noted earlier that current scholarship on black churches is hampered by a shortage of reliable statistical data.[76]

The importance of this monumental work is best highlighted on the back cover of the book. The Black Church in America has long been recognized as the most independent, stable, and dominant institution in black communities. Based on a ten-year study, The Black Church in the African American Experience is the largest nongovernmental survey of urban and rural churches ever undertaken and the first major field study since the thirties. Drawing on interviews with more than 1,800 black clergy in both urban and rural settings, combined with a comprehensive historical overview of seven mainline black denominations, C. Eric Lincoln and Lawrence H. Mamiya

---

[76]Lincoln and Mamiya, *The Black Church in the African American Experience*, 93.

present an analysis of the Black Church as it relates to the history of African Americans and to contemporary black culture. In examining both the internal structure of the Church and the reactions of the Church to external, societal challenges, the authors provide important insights into the Church's relationship to politics, economics, women, youth, and music, and trends that will define the Black Church well into the next century.

In conclusion of the literature review, this author has some observations to make as it relates to the lack of available data. First, in the history of the African American church, you wrestle with a lack of scholarship as it relates to writing. In other words, not too many African Americans are involved in the study and research of this field of study. Secondly, in the beginning of the African American church in America, a great deal of history was not recorded. This lack of recording was due to limited reading and writing skills. Also, as it relates to retrieving accurate and honest facts or data, there appears to be almost a code of silence of sorts among African American pastors in the majority of rural churches. Therefore, gaining information on budgets, bodies, and buildings becomes a challenge. Finally, the writings that pertain to African American pastors and churches by those outside the African American community are often skewed because of outsider's inability to get inside and obtain the whole truth.

As one views the current literature, there is hope of drastic improvements in information over the next several decades. We are in an incredible age of technology and education opportunities and because of this, more studies will be done and more information will come available in the future. As more walls of the past are broken down, as more and more racial reconciliation takes place, and as more African Americans become educated and go into this field of study, we will have an emergence of information pertaining to the unique challenges of African American pastors of small churches in the South.

CHAPTER 4

THE AUTHOR'S RESEARCH

The *World Book Encyclopedia* defines the South as a region in the United States that consists of the following States: Alabama, Arkansas, Delaware, Florida, Georgia, Kentucky, Louisiana, Maryland, Mississippi, North Carolina, South Carolina, Tennessee, Virginia, and West Virginia.[77] For the purpose of this thesis, the focus will be on the unique challenges of African American pastors in the Deep South: Mississippi, Arkansas, Louisiana, Georgia, and Alabama, excluding metropolitan areas in the Deep South such as New Orleans or Atlanta, etc. This author realizes there are similarities of African American pastors in small churches outside this region. This particular study will have a high concentration of subjects located in the Deep South rural areas and smaller counties.

To discover the unique challenges of African American

---

[77] World Book Encyclopedia, s.v. "United States," by John Edwin Coffman and Teresa A. Sullivan.

pastors of small churches in the South, the following approach was taken by this author. First, there was a survey given that involved African Americans and non-African Americans. Secondly, there was a focus group meeting held to discuss the various viewpoints of African Americans and non-African Americans. Third, there were conversations held with African Americans and non-African Americans. Fourth, there was a comparison made between two different authors who were writing about the work of pastors and congregations. One of the works comes from a non-African American author who wrote about and studied mostly non-African American pastors and congregations, and the other study for comparison comes from an African American who studied, exclusively, African American pastors and congregations. Finally, in a class done on small churches and congregations, a survey was given to the students to get their input on the subject of the unique challenges of African American pastors of small churches in the South.

The information and the results of the survey are as follows: The survey was sent to 119 pastors in the South. The survey had the option of anonymity. The document covered information such as the educational level of the pastor, the leadership and vision of the church, the congregational expectations of the pastor, the pastoral expectations, questions of size, questions of race, and other miscellaneous information. There was a 31% response rate to the survey. The percentage of response is a fact of attestation to this author's belief that it is hard to get information from pastors and churches to conduct a survey and have a true composite picture of what is happening among pastors and congregations. Of the responses, there were 31 responses from African Americans and 6 responses from non-African Americans.

First, as it relates to education, the survey revealed that as a whole, white clergy had more education, both general and theological, than black clergy. All the white participants of the survey had completed some form of education beyond high school. Of the six white ministers: two had bachelor's degrees, two had completed at least two years of college, and two had master's degrees. This education was not specifically in the area of religious studies. Of the African Americans surveyed, seven participants or 22% had only a high school education. The other numbers are as follows: seven people reported having a bachelor's degree, five pastors reported having at least gone to college for two years, four pastors reported having earned a master's degree, and four pastors reported having a doctorate degree. Another interesting note is that the majority of African American pastors reporting educational accomplishments in the area of Religion beyond the high school level earned these degrees from non-accredited agencies. This shows a trend of African American pastors attempting to become more educated but doing it through non-traditional means.

Another result of the survey comes in the area of income levels for the churches pastored. All the white pastors reported income levels above one hundred thousand dollars. One church had over one million dollars income. One church reported income in excess of two hundred thousand dollars, with the remaining four churches income being greater than one hundred thousand dollars. For the African American congregations, seventeen of the thirty-one, or fifty-five percent had incomes of less than one hundred thousand dollars. Four churches showed income of between one hundred thousand and two hundred thousand dollars. Five churches reported income of between two hundred thousand and three hundred thousand dollars. One church had an income between three hundred thousand and four hundred thousand dollars. Two churches reported income of between four hundred thousand and five hundred thousand dollars. Finally, one church reported income in excess of one million dollars. Based on the overall percentages, African Americans have less money in their churches than their white counterparts.

In the area of tenure in the position of pastor, it was shown that the average tenure of white pastors was seven years compared to black pastors with thirteen years. This can be an indication that having more finances is not an indication of stability as it relates to the position of pastor. Also, a greater number of African American pastors were involved in non-traditional churches which often they had started. This, of course, would account for them sometimes staying in the position of pastor longer than their white counterparts.

In the survey, there were some questions relating to leadership and vision. When asked, "Who determines what happens to the finances in your church or who establishes the budget," no white pastors reported having control over this area. On the other hand, there were ten African American pastors who said they were in control when it comes to finances and budgets. Also, when asked concerning vision both white and black pastors stated the vision of the church was determined by them.

Concerning the biggest challenges faced by pastors, the majority of both white and black clergy stated the challenge as being, "commitment from church members." For the African American pastor, next to commitment from church members, finances were listed as the biggest challenge in churches. For the white pastors, finances were not even on the list of challenges by these participants of the survey. Perhaps, hand in hand with finances, all six white pastors reported working full time in ministry as opposed to black ministers in which only sixty-one percent reported working full time in ministry.

Another note was in the area of attendance to weekly activities. The African American churches had a higher Sunday morning average worship attendance than their white counterparts. African Americans averaged 190 people during Sunday morning worship with whites averaging 151 attendees. Pertaining to Sunday night service, 83% of whites held night service with an average attendance of 117, compared to only 16% of blacks with seventy-eight people in attendance. Sunday school attendance showed whites averaging 122 people compared to blacks showing an average of sixty-five people. Finally, the midweek prayer/Bible study showed the African American churches having an average of fifty-five people, compared to whites having an average of ninety-four people in attendance. To put it succinctly, based on the numbers, African Americans come to church in a big way for Sunday worship and then the numbers fade out for other worship opportunities compared to whites whose numbers are a lot higher for the other opportunities of worship.

As it relates to different challenges of pastors from different races, for the white pastors five of the six stated there were no differences in the challenge of pastoring people. For the black pastors, 49% stated they felt like there was a different challenge as it relates to white pastors. When asked what those challenges were the answers were such things as economic positioning better for whites, education level greater for whites, history of races different, mentality different for races, attitude of worship different in the races, following leadership better in white congregations, blacks having less pastoral care resources, support from the community greater for whites, black churches not being as resourced as white churches, white churches having more staff, white churches having more knowledge in the area of health education, etc. This is a list of the more pronounced differences without repeating. It is important to note that the above listings are direct quotes from the survey which was based on what people thought, not necessarily on what they could scientifically prove.

Finally, as it relates to staffing, there was not much difference shown. African American churches in the survey averaged three full-time employees and two part-time employees compared to whites who showed having three full-time employees and three part-time employees on average. Something must be said in respect to musicians, who most African American pastors in the South would probably count as being full time if they play the instrument each Sunday. On the other hand, most white churches would count musicians as full time if they are receiving a full-time salary and that is their only employment.

The second part of the research project involved doing a random focus group meeting. The meeting involved a discussion with three African American pastors and one non-African American pastor.

The focus group discussion involved seven questions:

1. How many conferences, workshops, or trainings have you attended in the last 3 years?

> How many were led by African American leadership?
>
> How many were in the South? Alabama, Arkansas, Louisiana, Mississippi?
>
> How many had a comparably sized membership to your church?

2. What are your 3 biggest personal concerns as a pastor?

3. What are your 3 biggest church concerns, presently?

4. When needing to get/know information from other pastors, do you find it hard to get?

5. What do you think are some of the unique challenges faced by African American Pastors of small churches in the South?

6. What are your top 3 frustrations as a pastor?

7. Do you have any formal accountability in place for yourself as it relates to the ministry?

The results of the discussion that concerns this author are here recorded. In regards to question one, concerning the number and location of conferences or trainings attended, it was discovered that both groups attended about the same number of trainings or conferences, and the majority of the ones attended did not have comparable membership sizes. The number of conferences attended in the last two years by both races was six. It is also noted that half of the trainings were held or attended in the South.

As it relates to the biggest personal concerns of these pastors, the same concerns surfaced on both sides of the racial divide. The biggest concerns were personal health and being successful in the calling of ministry. An interesting note was that finances was mentioned as a personal concern for the non-African American pastor and finances was not mentioned at all for African American pastors present in the discussion. This is the opposite of what was reported on the survey given to pastors.

In respect to the third discussion, which was about the biggest church concerns these pastors faced, the following is noted. Each participant listed growth of the church as a top concern in the church. Also, a lack of commitment from church members was a huge issue among both races. In the group discussion it was mentioned how one measures success and how the media plays a role in how we view and measure our own success. To put this part of the discussion more bluntly, it was discussed that success should not be measured in terms of buildings, bodies, and budgets. With this in mind, it was felt that many ministers are being influenced by these false measures of success and a lot of it stems from television ministry and major conferences in which this attitude and viewpoint becomes the dominant perspective that is given and received. This is not to say that these impressions are given intentionally.

The fourth discussion involved the transmission of helpful information from other pastors or leaders. In this discussion, the non-African American pastors stated they would not have any problem getting or giving private information from others; mainly because their view was one of teamwork. For the African American, one pastor stated they would not have any problem getting or giving information from other pastors. Another pastor stated he would have problems giving private information to others because of the issue of confidentiality. His belief was that among preachers, keeping things confidential was a major issue. Also, he stated difficulty in getting helpful information from other pastors due to their personal ambitions at being number one or for some other personal status reasons.

As it relates to the fifth discussion, the question was, "What do you think are some of the unique challenges faced by African American Pastors of small churches in the South?" It is interesting that for this question, all those present including the non-African American thought the issue of having to deal with traditions in the church was a unique challenge. Also, getting major, consistent support and commitment from the membership were listed as a unique challenge of African American pastors of small churches in the South. In addition to the above-mentioned items, one pastor discussed the difficulty of introducing new things in the congregation as a serious challenge. In this author's opinion, this would go hand in hand with tradition and the hold that tradition can have on people being willing to accept new concepts or ideas.

The sixth discussion involved the top frustrations of pastors. Both black and white pastors stated the maturity level of church members as a frustration point to combat. Another top frustration that the white pastor discussed was church members misunderstanding the role of the Pastor. Finally, the African American pastors listed people not cooperating with the vision and visionary of the church as a top frustration in the African American church community.

The final discussion question was, "Do you have any formal accountability in place for yourself as it relates to the ministry?" None of the African American pastors had formal accountability in place. On the other hand, the non-African American pastor did have accountability in place. All of the pastors stated they had informal accountability in place with their peers.

The third part of the research to determine the unique challenges of African American pastors of small churches in the south involved personal interviews with both races. The interview questions were informal but involved general discussions on challenges faced by pastors. The one challenge that was consistent among all African American pastors was having the finances to do adequate ministry. The consistent theme of non-African American pastors was people's commitment to the church. In the informal interviews, all the pastors shared a genuine burden for the Lord's church and all the pastors shared a genuine desire for their churches to grow.

The fourth part of the research to determine the unique challenges faced by African American pastors of small churches in the South is a comparison made between two different authors who were writing about the work of pastors and congregations. On the side of the non-African Americans two books were viewed in the literary review, *Congregations in America* by Mark Chaves and *God's Potters* by Jackson W. Carroll. These authors' research involved mostly non-African American pastors and congregations. To be more specific about the statement, "mostly non-African American pastors and congregations," the statistics will bear this point out. In the book, *Congregations in America*, 1236 congregations were viewed and only 11.9% were African Americans.[78] In the book, *God's Potters*, 832 pastors were surveyed and only 15% were African American.[79] On the other side, for comparison, we will view another book highlighted in the literary review, *The Black Church in the African American Experience* by C. Eric Lincoln and Lawrence H. Mamiya. The latter author's research involves only African American pastors and their congregations.

In the books, *God's Potters* and *The Black Church in the African American Experience*, the comparison will focus on the ending of each book. In *God's Potters,* the last two chapters focus on excellence and how to achieve it. Those two chapters are namely, "A Manner of Life Worthy of the Gospel, and Strengthening Pastoral Leadership and Nurturing Excellence: Some Strategies." In *God's Potters*, the writer appears to be saying, "Here is how you can move from good to great." There is an assumption that the foundation for excellence in ministry has already been laid and simply needs to be built on top of and or perfected. On the other hand, in *The Black Church in the African American Experience*, as the authors conclude the book they appear to be saying, "you've started as a church but now there is a need to become solidly established."

As we delve into how the books are concluded first we look at *God's Potters*. The author states, "Despite the complexity that various contexts introduce, we can lift up some characteristics or marks of excellent ministry that seem to exemplify it in many different settings. While they do not

---

[78] Mark Chaves, *Congregations in America*, 218/223.
[79] Jackson W. Carroll. *God's Potters*, 245/275.

exhaust the possibilities, they are characteristics that, from our discussions and focus group interviews, I have come to believe are of special importance for any ministry that aims at a Christ-shaped excellence in the face of particular contextual challenges."[80] In the pages that follow this author lists those characteristics as follows: resiliency and spiritual disciplines, agility and reflective leadership, trust and personal authority, staying connected, and self-directed, career-long learning.[81]

Now to examine the conclusion in the book, *The Black Church in the African American Experience*, the authors offer an unscientific postscript, entitled "Policy recommendations for the Black Church." The following is offered by the authors,

> After delving into the scholarly literature on the history, sociology, and demographics of black churches and black communities, and after traveling thousands of miles, crisscrossing the United States in pursuit of interviews with black clergy in rural and urban churches, large and small, the sense of the spiritual and cultural munificence with which the Black Church has endowed the lives and experiences of black people, past and present, is inescapable. Black churches are not perfect institutions but with all their limitations they represent the institutionalized staying power of a human community that has been under siege for close to four hundred years. Black personalities,

---

[80] Ibid., 205.
[81] Ibid., 206-218.

movements, and ideologies have waxed and waned over the years and will continue to do so, but black churches have remained a firm anchor stabilizing the black experience and giving it meaning through the uncertain eras of change and counter-change. Nevertheless, there are areas of proper concern for the Black Church, just as there are for any prudent institution that cares about a future of service and relevance. Some conclusions we reached have already been suggested by other researchers, and their consideration is already on the agenda of some churches. Others are not as obvious and probably require a kind of self-study or inventory by the churches themselves before the full impact of existing or portending problems can be assessed.[82]

After this, the authors list four powerful recommendations for the African American Church. Those recommendations listed are the need for a better-trained and better-educated clergy, improved benefits for black clergy, and the problem of understaffing for black churches, and black families in general.[83]

As noted earlier, the point of the comparison from these two major studies is that they are from two different perspectives. The African American pastor and the non-African American pastor are at different points in respect to their history and development. A white pastor may be focused on resiliency and spiritual disciplines while a black

---

[82] Lincoln and Mamiya, *The Black Church in the African American Experience*, 398-399.
[83] Ibid., 399–404.

pastor or denominational leader could be focused on simply finding staff for basic operations. A white pastor could be focused on agility and reflective leadership, while a black pastor could be focused on the overwhelming negative plight of the families in the neighborhood. A white pastor could be focused on self-directed, career-long learning, while a black pastor could be focused on just initial basic seminary training. A white pastor could be focused on staying connected, while a black pastor could be focused on trying to get basic pastoral benefits to be connected in a full-time capacity with the church.

The final investigation, by this author, was conducting a class on Pastors and Small Congregations in the South. The class involved a lecture, some discussions, and a survey. The class was a course taught at the New Life Fellowship School of Ministry in Columbia and McComb, MS. It involved over fifty students, thirty-three of whom participated in the survey, out of which only one was white. The survey was similar to the one given to Pastors, although the class involved both pastors and non-pastors. There were a number of questions asked, with this author being concerned with the one question related to dealing with the unique challenges faced by African American pastors.

The questions during this exercise were not posed to do a comparison, but rather to gather input as to what people thought concerning race and different challenges faced by different races. The first question asked was, "Do you feel that your challenges as a church are different than those of other races?" The second question was, "What challenges do you feel exist, as it relates to another race?" The result from the question about the challenges being different was the following: four people did not respond; nineteen people thought there were different challenges; nine people thought the challenges were not any different. As it relates to what people thought were different, the following are some of the answers: as blacks we have a different outlook, the economics are different, educational levels are different, whites are more prejudiced than blacks, one person felt that blacks, in general, have a lack of education in studying and interpreting the Word of God, one comment dealt with the difference in culture; one person felt that community and business involvement was better for whites, another person felt that it was better for whites at getting approved for loans, another comment was that it was easier for whites to get committed church members.

All of the above comments may beg for commentary and further discussion. This author or this paper's readers may not agree with the responses, but there are certain facts that are obvious. First, the majority of people think there are different challenges. (In this survey, 57% thought the challenges were different). Secondly, the opinions have a wide range: moving from being very strong to very controversial, and even to being unsubstantiated and perhaps bordering along the lines of pure myths. Whatever one may think, the opinions are yet there and they are a factor in the unique challenges faced by African American pastors of small churches in the South.

In view of this author's research on the unique challenges of African American pastors of small churches in the South, it is perhaps interesting that all pastors, African Americans and non-African Americans, had some challenges that were common to all, but the order of their focus was different. As an example, most pastors had finances as a challenge but the majority of the white pastors listed this challenge as not a main concern, as opposed to most blacks who, in most cases, had it as their number one challenge. If it was not the pastor's number one challenge, the challenge listed could be solved if the pastor had the proper amount of finances.

From the study done by this author, this chapter concludes with the succinct unique challenges faced by African American pastors of small churches in the South. In this author's opinion, the number one challenge is that of overcoming the negative effect and impact of history on the

African American pastor and on the African American church in respect to slavery and oppression. Out of this number one challenge, there are sub-challenges that are directly or indirectly tied to the issue of slavery and oppression. The sub-challenges are: 1) overcoming the educational barriers that exist in the South rising out of segregation, 2) dealing with the economic issues of the south rising out of racism, 3) breaking the mindset of slavery and poverty in the African American thought process, and 4) living and worshiping around the residue of the past injustices.

It is not just unique to this author to show other problems stemming from one problem. In the introduction of the book, *Putting the Movement Back into Civil Rights Teaching*, we find the following by James Boggs and Grace Lee Boggs:

> The first thing we have to understand is that racism is not a "mental quirk" or a "psychological flaw" on an individual's part. Racism is the systematized oppression by one race of another. In other words, it is the various forms of oppression within every sphere of social relations-- economic exploitation, military subjugation, political subordination, cultural devaluation, psychological violation, sexual degradation, verbal abuse, etc.—that together make up the interaction and developing processes which operate so normally and naturally, and are so much a part of the existing institutions of the society, that the individuals involved are barely conscious of their operation.[84]

---

[84] Putting the Movement Back into Civil Rights Teaching,

This assessment highlights the issue that slavery and oppression have a far-reaching impact on any people, far beyond simply the negative act that occurred in the past.

The second challenge is listed in connection with a point made by Anthony B. Pinn. In his writings, there is a discussion of how the black church was closely aligned with the black community and the social issues of that early era. He states, "This blending of social protest and Christian faith resulted in many scholars, preachers, and laypeople thinking of the Black Church and black communities as intimately connected. This points to an important and historical intertwining of the Black Church's development and the needs of black Americans, which probably hit its twentieth-century high point with the civil rights movement."[85] In the post-civil rights era it appears now that the gap between the black community and the black church is growing even wider, which is the second major unique challenge that the African American pastor has particularly in the South; the challenge of connecting and keeping people in church who are living in the shadow of a church that was so tied to the problems of the community.

The third challenge, in this author's opinion, is an issue tied to successful large churches in larger cities and larger suburban areas. This challenge is developing and maintaining a healthy church in the South which may not be a huge church. The connection of the larger churches, as it relates to unique challenges, is its influence on the smaller churches in urban areas. With the advancement of

---

(Washington, D.C.: Teaching for Change and the Poverty & Race Research Action Council, 2004), 20.

[85] Ibid., 18.

technology and the ease of 21st-century travel, smaller churches and pastors of smaller churches in rural areas are fully aware of the growth and prosperity of the larger churches and these larger churches often create the standard or the model to be envied.

The fourth and final unique challenge of African American pastors of small churches in the South is simply being able to transition from irrelevant traditions. Traditions such as pastoral selections based on a person's ability to 'hoop,' or having fundraisers instead of tithing income, or having pastors reporting to deacons, or paying pastors substandard wages, are all such traditions there are referenced. This author is aware that these traditions are not true of all churches in the South.

This challenge focuses mainly on the African American pastor having to deal with congregations that are heavily tied to traditions and often are not easy to be transitioned from them. There were some traditions that were developed along the way during the beginning of the African American church in the South which are no longer relevant to the time in which we now live. It is not just the tradition itself but it is also the culture that the tradition creates.

CHAPTER 5

SUGGESTED MINISTRY BASED ON THE UNIQUE CHALLENGES

After being made aware of the unique challenges faced by African American pastors of small churches in the South, the question now becomes, "How does one minister in respect to such a context?" This question should not just concern the African American pastor of a small church in the South but it should also concern others as well. How to minister in this context should concern the non-African American pastor in the South and North, who will need to teach and preach on healing the wounds of past injustices in their congregations and to their constituents. How to minister in this context should concern the pastors of large churches who hold trainings and conferences that are attended by the small church pastor. How to minister in this context should concern the members of small churches in the South who visit larger churches and or view them through some media form. How to minister in this context should concern the members of large churches who visit a smaller congregation. In some form or another, these relationships can serve to heal or hinder the ministry of the unique challenges of African American pastors of small churches in the South.

As the attention turns to suggestions on how to minister in this context, this writer would like to first discuss how to minister in general. The Bible is full of racial, social, economic, political, and moral issues in which Jesus taught people how to minister. The first contention of this author for all Christians is to simply observe and obey the commands of the Word of God and to turn to the Holy Scriptures in order to secure a foundation for ministry.

John 3:16 states, "For God so loved the world that he gave his only begotten Son, that whosoever believeth in him should not perish but have everlasting life." First John 3:8 states, "For this purpose the Son of God was manifested, that he might destroy the works of the devil." Second Peter 3:9 argues, "The Lord is not slack concerning his promise, as some men count slackness; but is longsuffering to us-ward, not willing that any should perish, but that all should come to repentance." Romans 3:23 says, "For all have sinned, and come short of the glory of God." First John 1:9 says, "If we confess our sins, he is faithful and just to forgive us our sins, and to cleanse us from all unrighteousness." First John 4:7 exhorts, "Beloved, let us love one another: for love is of God; and every one that loveth is born of God, and knoweth God." Second Corinthians 5:20 proclaims, "Now then we are ambassadors for Christ, as though God did beseech you by us: we pray you in Christ's stead, be ye reconciled to God." The point of these scriptures is to note that basic ministry must be foundational to all unique ministry contexts. If, in fact, foundational ministry is done it will cover all ministry contexts. The unique ministry contexts will simply cause us to build on top of what has been foundational. The premise of basic ministry based on the above scriptures is love, forgiveness, and reconciliation which are available to all and for all. If the above truths are preached, believed and applied in all churches among all races of people, healing will become the inevitable.

Keeping in mind the basics of ministry, it would now be appropriate to offer suggested ways of ministry in respect to the unique challenges noted. In this author's opinion, the number one challenge is that of overcoming the negative effect and impact of history on the African American pastor and on the African American church in respect to slavery and oppression. First, there cannot be any erasing or ignoring of the past from the white community and/or others. Also, there cannot be the constant dwelling on the past by the African American community. Though not always easy, the past must be dealt with from a sensitive posture on both sides of the racial divide of black and white.

This author's suggestion is to always see this part of history through the eyes of the teachings of Christ. When Zacchaeus had a conversion encounter with Christ in Luke chapter nineteen, he became willing to share what he had with those who were without. The next thing he does is to acknowledge the wrong he has perpetuated on other people. But not only does he acknowledge his wrong, he also becomes willing to make restitution for the wrong that was done.[86] To put it plainly, the white community should consider dealing with the past by first acknowledging it and then become willing to rectify its wrongs. The article "The Wealth Gap Widens," by Chuck Collins in *Dollars and Sense* magazine (September/October 1999) talks about the disparity between whites and blacks as it relates to wealth and gives some hard truthful data for consideration. One of the more interesting points in the article is this note:

> The racial wealth gap reflects the reality that wealth accumulation occurs over generations, as parents pass on assets to their children in the form of home ownership, savings, and estates. Past and present

---

[86] Luke 19:1-10 KJV.

racial discrimination in asset-building, including slavery, Jim Crow laws, discriminatory employment, insurance, and bank lending practices, have kept many people of color from getting on the asset-building train.[87]

For those in the African American community, in overcoming the past, forgiveness becomes a Christian principle that must be practiced. In Luke chapter 23 we find Jesus hanging on the cross as a result of the sin and evil in people. Also, during this time we hear him say, "Father, forgive them; for they know not what they do."[88] As hard as this issue may be for the African American community, there is a powerful example in Jesus Christ. Forgiveness is one of the first steps in overcoming such a horrible injustice as slavery and oppression.

Next, a look at the suggested ministry recommendations in light of the sub-challenges flowing out of the main challenge will be taken, namely, overcoming the negative effect and impact of history on the African American pastor and on the African American church in respect to slavery and oppression. For the sub-challenge— overcoming the educational barrier that exists in the South rising out of segregation—this author offers the following: African American pastors must make the education of themselves and those in their congregations a high priority. Also, congregations seeking pastors should give special considerations to those who have excelled in religious

---

[87] Putting the Movement Back into the Civil Rights Movement, 451.

[88] Luke 23:34 KJV.

academia. The authors Lincoln and Mamiya offer similar sentiments in their comments:

> The ministry of the Black Church is the only profession where only one out of every four or five practitioners has graduated from professional school. Professional education will help enhance the skills and effectiveness of black clergy not only in the areas of spiritual nurture, theological understanding, biblical interpretation, preaching, and counseling, but also in financial accountability and economic development, record keeping, and political awareness and moral responsibility.[89]

These authors further add comments that are both reflective of the past and at the same time the comments help to direct us toward a bright future in the field of education:

The evangelical traditions of the past which set the norm for the emergent black denominations only required evidence of a sincere call from God to the ministry. A prudent policy for the future would add professional education and a full-time clergy to that norm. The inherent fractures of life in the black community will increasingly require full-time attention from professionals fully prepared to give counsel, leadership, and succor in an era in which the traditional reservoir of humanitarian concern are increasingly depleted.[90]

---

[89] Lincoln and Mamiya, *The Black Church in the African American Experience*, 399.
[90] Ibid., 400.

Suggested ministry in respect to the second sub-challenge, namely, dealing with the economic issues of the south rising out of racism, is the following: Inasmuch as substantial wealth is built over a number of generations, it is suggested that pastors and churches begin to make decisions with future generations in mind. Pastors and churches should make conscious attempts to build wealth for the next generation and not just focus on what the current generation needs. Simple things to accomplish would be passing on clear assets as opposed to passing on debt, obtaining and maintaining good life insurance policies, the establishments of wills and trusts that include not only family but church organizations as well, and the training of children and church members in the area of good financial stewardship. The execution of such practices will help to improve the gap which was noted by Anthony B. Pinn, in *The Black Church in the Post-Civil Rights Era*: "In 1995, the median income of all Afro-American families was $25,970, which was 60.8 percent of the Euro-American median family income of $42,646. This was only a 1.6 percent improvement on the ratio of 59.2 percent in 1967."[91]

Finally, as it relates to economics, if serious and immediate attention is not given to the issue of economics, a reverse effect will occur. This reverse effect is that if there is not improved economics in the African American community there will inevitably be an economic drain on existing churches. Hozell C. Francis in *Church Planting in the African American Context* states, "As economic and social problems continue to afflict the African-American community, affected families will reach out to the black church for help.

---

[91] Pinn, *The Black Church in the Post-Civil Rights Era*, 74.

Church leaders must understand the devastation that economic paucity brings to the families in the church community."[92] It must be noted that poor people, in terms of economic wealth and prosperity, will lead to poor churches and when poor people go to poor churches for help, the church will become even poorer or in most cases will not be positioned to offer assistance.

Suggested ministry for the third sub-challenge, which is breaking the mindset of slavery and poverty in the African American thought process, is the following: Pastors must make consistent and deliberate attempts at reshaping the minds of the youth through targeted teaching and exposure of a better life. Because it will, realistically, take a number of generations to become loosed from the tyranny of the past, this author proposes for the youth and children to become the target of teaching. Also, it must be considered that a large portion of the present day adult population remains too close to the pain and impact of the past to become fully free, notwithstanding what adults may allow God to do.

In the book, *Think and Grow Rich: A Black Choice*, Dennis Kimbro says, "The pattern of your thinking today is transforming your tomorrows."[93] It was Thoreau who wrote, "If one advances confidently in the direction of his dreams and endeavors to live the life he has imagined, he will meet success unexpected in common hours."[94]

---

[92] Hilliard, *Church Planting in the African American Context*, 86.
[93] Dennis Kimbro and Napoleon Hill, *Think and Grow Rich: A Black Choice*, (New York: Fawcett Books, 1991), 77.
[94] Ibid., 78.

Examples of doing targeted things to change the thinking of young people is insisting on quality education for all, consistently displaying positive role models along their paths, doing classes that promote upward mobility, exposing youth to other cultures through trips and through media, insisting that kids become great readers, and investing dollars in tangible, relevant youth programs.

When one looks back and remembers what led to the historic Brown vs. Board of Education, it must be concluded that strong, consistent teaching in the area of self-identify, self-esteem, and racial identity is of utmost importance. The account is as follows:

> From 1939 until the early 1950s the husband and wife team of black psychologists Drs. Kenneth and Mamie Clark published a series of studies on the racial self-identification of black children. These studies played an important role in the 1954 Supreme Court decision in the celebrated Brown v. Board of Education case which desegregated public schools. The case, which was brought by Leon Oliver Brown, pastor of the St. Mark's A.M.E. Church in Topeka, Kansas, and the NAACP Legal Defense Fund on behalf of nine-year-old Linda Brown and other black children, used the results of the doll-choice tests developed by the Clarks to show the detrimental effects of a segregated and inferior school system on black children. According to the Clarks, 67 percent of the black children preferred to play with a white doll but 66 percent of them also identified with the black doll. However,

they concluded that the 34 percent of black youngsters who did not identify with the black doll suffered from low self-esteem.[95]

Living and worshiping around the residue of the past injustices is the last sub-challenge we view. Suggested ministry for this sub-challenge is one for much personal reflection. This author suggests that, whether you are black or white, one honestly go before God and be specific about the issue being addressed and ask God for healing and deliverance. To the intellectual person this suggestion may seem like simple spiritual hype, but to the sincere child of God, it is the Word of God to His people, whom he really loves. If this suggestion is believed and practiced, it will move one in the direction of healing.

Also, the suggested ministry for this challenge is for African Americans and non-African Americans to make deliberate attempts at worshipping together. Even though united worship may not take place every Sunday, it should take place. Even though all races are different, there are numerous areas where everyone has the same goals or objectives. Hozell C. Francis weighs in on this thought process with the following:

> There are numerous areas where blacks and whites have similar aspirations. For example, most of us desire success in our careers, and we want our children to grow up and make a contribution to society; we are concerned about owning our homes

---

[95] Lincoln and Mamiya, *The Black Church in the African American Experience*, 313.

and growing up spiritually. Conversely, there are generalized differences between black and whites. Often there are measurable variations in music appreciation, art, dance, vernacular, dress, etc. Evidently these differences have their origin in our histories. Nevertheless, they affect the way we are and act in every aspect of life. The church is not immune to these distinctives. Indeed, they are evident in many facets of church life. It is conceivable that there will be a continuing market for the individualized expression of the differences we have. However, a significant number of persons can be equipped to work in tandem for progress and to go beyond the confines of cultural restraints.[96]

Francis, in his writings concerning the homogeneous principle in the African American Churches, states, "When people get to know one another in more intimate ways, they will respect and accept one another for who they really are."[97] The term homogeneous simply means similar in nature or structure.[98]

The second unique challenge faced by African American pastors of small churches in the South is connecting and keeping people in church who are living in the shadow of a church that was so tied to the problems of the community. Suggested ministry for this challenge is for the African

---

[96] Hilliard, *Church Planting in the African American Context*, 17-18.

[97] Ibid., 103.

[98] *Websters Tower Dictionary*. (Cleveland: The World Publishing Company, 1954), 139.

American pastor to re-think the church's purpose, focus, programs, and preaching context. There must be great reflection on where one is going more than on where one has been. In the beginning of the African American church in the United States, church was all the African Americans really owned. The African American church became the center of the African American community, especially as it relates to the people's response to problems and injustices perpetuated on African Americans as a whole. The observation of Hozell C. Francis was noted during this author's thought process. He says, "The black church has played a comprehensive and multi-faceted role in its community. Primarily this has been necessary because many avenues for social, economic, and political expressions were closed to African-American. The future of the development of society in politics and economics will determine how important the church's traditional role will continue to be. As blacks and other minorities become assimilated into society at large, the multifaceted role of the church may lessen."[99]

When the African American church started and began to grow, up until the early 1970's the social issues of our society seemed to have the major role in the African American church. So, people during this era came to church, predominantly because the church solved their social problems. There was not the fitting into the mainstream of society, so people came to church to find and express their sociological needs. When there were injustices done to African Americans in the community, they came to the church and the church went back into the

---

[99] Francis, *Church Planting in the African American Context*, 76.

community and addressed the problem.

In dealing with the origins of the foundation of the African American church, each pastor must celebrate and appreciate the origins, but also must begin to switch the foundation and focus from the social to the spiritual aspects. In other words, as the church started, it was primarily a catalyst for addressing the social issues in the black community and then moving to the spiritual issues. The African American community must see the spiritual need of people as the primary issue and allow this aspect of ministry to become foundational to why one needs the church in his or her life. As society has developed, more and more agencies in communities that deal with injustices and other civil rights issues have established. This truth has led to a choice; people can use the church or other agencies to address civil rights issues. This author strongly states that every person needs Jesus and a church family in which to live out his or her Christian faith. This view will make the church relevant for all times and seasons.

One of the main ways that the African American pastor of small churches in the South can get at the heart of this issue (connecting and keeping people in church who are living in the shadow of a church that was so tied to the problems of the community) is through the pulpit presentation on Sunday mornings. Two notes about preaching for change is here, highlighted in this discussion. One remark concerning preaching comes from Hozell who properly noted, "As pastors in the black church develop a philosophy of preaching, it is most essential that they be concerned about not compromising when it comes to interpretation.

Theology need not be black or white, for when properly understood, the Bible speaks of fairness to all people."[100]

The other note this author makes on preaching is a suggestion that the African American preaching becomes more balanced to include an equal portion of encouragement and advancement. In a comment about the origin of African American preaching, Hozell makes this observation: "The tradition of black preaching developed in a context of dire circumstances. The need to engender a degree of hope in a climate of despair led to a particular kind of preaching."[101] Because of the oppressive climate at that time, there was a strong need to encourage people to "hold on" or "don't let go," or "keep the faith." These things were definitely warranted and still warranted today. But the recommendation is for there to be messages that will advance people from where they are to the next level or stage in their spiritual, personal, and social lives. An example of going from encouragement to advancement would be a message on "How to thrive" and not just "How to survive."

The third unique challenge faced by African American pastors of small churches in the South is developing and maintaining a healthy church, even though it may not be a huge church. This challenge can, indeed, be felt by all small churches. But for purposes of this paper, this author will offer suggestive ministry from an African American perspective. As stated earlier, because of the advancement of technology and the ease of travel, most people in smaller

---

[100] Ibid., 65.
[101] Ibid., 62.

churches are aware of the perceived success of larger churches. This author proposes to have open, informative communication on churches in general rather than negative discussions or no discussions. On the negative side, often pastors in smaller churches are faced with the challenge of people in their churches and the pastors, themselves, being influenced by the small amount of mega-churches, which are churches generally numbering into the thousands in membership. The reaction can range from a pastor of a smaller church being jealous or envious of larger churches to church members becoming depressed or having feelings of inadequacies due to a false perception that bigger is better.

From this challenge can be developed wonderful training, which when pastor and parishioner become engaged, can lead to good health in the small church. One such study could be simply, "understanding church growth." The opening illustration by Donald Hilliard Jr. in his book, *Church Growth from an African American Perspective*, could give invaluable insight; he opens his writings with the following:

> Over the past twenty years a significant change has occurred in the dynamic of African American church life: the emergence of the "megachurch." Prior to about 1980 the phenomenon of the local church with a membership in the thousands – though increasingly common in the Bible belt – was not a trend in the African American Christian community. In those days a black church with 500 members was considered a large church; a church of 1,000 or more was huge. The average church in America – black, white, or otherwise – had 85 to 125 members, a statistic that still holds true today, the increasing number of megachurches notwithstanding. Nevertheless, the recent appearance of black megachurches is forcing African American Christians to adjust their thinking about their churches and to reexamine what it

means to grow.[102]

In Glenn Daman's book, *Shepherding the Small Church*, he weighs in on the concept that all huge churches are not necessarily healthy and that a small church does not automatically equate to a church being unhealthy. Daman discusses a church being effective with the following:

> The vitality of a congregation is not found in its size or in its programs or budget. The vitality of a congregation is found in its fulfillment of God's purpose for the church. A church that has five thousand members and is growing may be just as unhealthy and ineffective as a church that has only fifty members and is declining. Conversely, a church with fifty members who are fulfilling God's mission can be as healthy and dynamic as a church with thousands of members. Churches do not close because they lack members and financial resources. Churches close when they are no longer being effective in fulfilling God's purposes for them.

Building an effective church begins with understanding the benchmarks for effectiveness. And the pastor and leadership must use these benchmarks to continually examine what the church is to be doing, how it is to do it, and why. Otherwise the congregation can easily become distracted by the pursuit of the insignificant.[103]

---

[102] Hilliard, *Church Growth from an African American Perspective*, 2.
[103] Daman, *Shepherding the Small Church*. 16.

Daman discusses how effectiveness is defined as it relates to the Bible. He also gives scriptural references as the proof-text for such discussion. He says the following: effectiveness is defined by transformation (Ephesians 4:12-13), effectiveness is defined by biblical and theological integrity (Ephesians 4:14), effectiveness is defined by faith (Ephesians 4:4-6), effectiveness is defined by relationship (Ephesians 4:1-6), effectiveness is defined by service (Ephesians 4:16), effectiveness is defined by relevancy (I Corinthians 9:19-23).[104]

The fourth and final unique challenge of African American pastors of small churches in the South is simply being able to transition from irrelevant traditions.

First, one must understand what tradition is and how tradition impacts the African American church. The dictionary defines tradition as oral transmission of events, opinions, doctrines, etc., through successive generations without written memorials.[105]

Traditions run especially deep in the African American Church community. The reason for this stronghold, as it relates to tradition, is that in the early years of the church, people could not read nor write. It would only make sense to pass things from one generation to the next in an oral manner. In the African American church, there were and are a lot of traditions that are held onto, religiously. This author's concern is not for the good traditions such as respect for adults, 'yes sir' or 'no sir' answers, speaking to

---

[104] Ibid., 18-20.
[105] Webster's Tower Dictionary, 272.

people as they pass by, taking one's neighbor food from the garden, letting the preacher eat first when invited to dinner, etc. The concern is for the traditions that are not scripturally based or no longer relevant to the time which we live.

Traditions such as the style of preaching, over the substance in preaching; or having annual days that fill up a calendar with little or no spiritual value, are examples of traditions from which the African American church and pastor must transition. Glenn Daman offers an excellent commentary and advice on understanding tradition in the small church. In chapter two of his book, *Shepherding the Small Church*, he lists fifteen characteristics of the small church. Characteristic seven is listed as, "Traditions and heritage undergird the structure, ministry, and culture." The following is said:

> Within the small church traditions are more than ruts; they are the stories and bonds that tie the present congregation to past generations. Because the small church values both past and current members, traditions play an important role in the life and expression of the church. The people tend to be slow to change, for change breaks apart what was constructed by past members. Each church has a story and each story has a human hero. New people need to learn the stories so they also can highly value the people behind them. Each church has sacred cows that are untouchable. They may be major issues, such as a particular program, or they may be as minor as the time of a service or the place of the pulpit. The reason they are sacred is because they connect to previous generations. The pulpit is sacred because it was built by Fred's great grandfather, one of the founders of the church. To replace the pulpit would be tantamount to forsaking the heritage of the church. The leaders need to identify these sacred cows, discern the

reasons they are important, and address needs for change sensitively.[106]

This author agrees with Daman that understanding and sensitivity is the key when attempting to transition from strong traditions. Suggested ministry in this situation will be to build new traditions and base them solely on the Word of God. As more traditions are built that are based on the Word of God and other relevant sound logic, it will cause the African American church to examine existing traditions in this new light. If it is seen by church members that certain traditions don't make good sense, they will become easier to discard. This fact will become true more for the next generation, which hopefully and respectfully, will be more educated than the previous.

---

[106]Daman, *Shepherding the Small Church*, 46-47.

CHAPTER 6

CONCLUSION

The conclusion to this study is four-fold: first, this author takes a final further look at the effect of history on the African American pastor in the South; second, there are comments made as to how the Church sees itself; third, the question is asked, "where do we go from here?"; and finally, there is a note of hope.

As have been discussed, there are also several factors that are unique to the African American pastors that may not be unique to others involved in the pastorate. Lawrence N. Jones makes the following statement:

> The underdevelopment of church structures and limited financial resources have also inhibited the growth of clergy retirement funds. Several denominations have made modest beginnings with pension programs, but most black pastors cannot afford to retire. Consequently, pastorates tend to

be marked by long tenure, and access is restricted for younger men and women. The difficulty in finding good placements has diminished the attractiveness of the ministry as a vocation for many promising young persons.[107]

This author concludes that the challenges faced by most African American pastors are strongly seated in the past. So, in the present, we have such challenges as how does an older pastor attract new young pastors to an entity that has some serious challenges to overcome such as limited resources, traditional strongholds, education and the realization that there is a problem? One such example that was highlighted focused on education. This need is critical in a religious community where an estimated 70 percent of the clergy lack formal theological education.[108] In an article on *Leaders for Black Churches,* the following was noted:

> In the Black Church in the African American Experience (1990), a landmark study of the seven major black denominations, C. Eric Lincoln and Lawrence Mamiya noted that black churches, while still viable and important, are struggling to address issues of racism, unemployment, child care, health care, housing, education, teen-age pregnancy, substance abuse, crime and violence while continuing to preach the gospel and tend to souls. "If we were asked to make a single policy recommendation that we consider critical for the

---

[107] Lawrence N. Jones, *The Black Churches: A New Agenda*, (Christian Century, http://newfirstsearch.oclc.org., 96 April 18, 1979), 436.
[108] Ibid., 435.

future of black churches, it would be the need for more, better-trained and better-educated clergy." At a time when black churches confront a widening gulf between middle-income blacks and the dependent poor, a rising number of unchurched among both groups, and generally better-educated people in the pews, preachers no longer can build churches and aid their communities through willpower alone. A seminary education, Lincoln and Mamiya explained, not only could deepen black pastors' theological understanding, biblical interpretation, preaching and counseling but also could strengthen them in areas of financial accountability, economic development, political awareness and moral responsibility. "The ideal black preachers," they said, "are able to combine the best formal education with the best of the black religious tradition." [109]

Although this powerful observation was made by noted scholars it has not been taken to heart by the black church as a whole, a large segment of which does not require pastors to have a college degree or formal theological education to be ordained.[110] Some leaders think that seminary education for black ministers has frequently been miseducation.[111] So now it can be easily detected that African American churches who have struggled with the very foundation of education from its conception, even

---

[109] Simmons, Charitey. *Leaders for black churches*, (Christian Century, http://web15.epnet.com/direct.asp?an=9502205665&db=rlh 1 February 95, Volume 112 Issue 4), 100.
[110] Ibid.
[111] Ibid.

today, struggle when its leaders are educated. This, in itself, is another unique challenge that is often wrestled with in the African American religious community.

John W. Kinney, dean of the School of Theology at Virginia Union University in Richmond, contends that some seminary programs have operated on "a principle of negation and denial" that conveys to black students that "what you bring, what you've been doing (in the local church), is wrong and now we've got to show you the right way to set up worship, the right way to sing, the right way to preach." When they returned to the black church, some of these seminary-trained pastors could no longer celebrate the gifts of their congregations. "They couldn't be with people," Kinney explained. "All they could do is judge and criticize."[112]

Another obvious effect of history on the African American pastor of today is that, since most churches came from poverty-stricken origins, that mentality still lingers in a number of African American communities and churches. If the churches as a whole are poor, usually the leadership is poor, especially if they are solely supported by the church. Insufficient money, in most cases, will equate to inadequate buildings, budgets, ministry impact, outreach, education, and sometimes vision. Even as churches do come into more money, there is yet the struggle for financial management, stewardship and accountability.

Furthermore, the African American pastor today is faced with trying to lead a church body that is proud to have

---

[112] Ibid.

something of its own without the influence of the white race. Coming out of an oppressive society and not having the opportunity to be in charge or to be valued in its community, the African American church is the place where a normal person can have a voice and a vote and be viewed as "somebody." The issue for some pastors in this situation is that a great number of people want to be leaders and want to have their expression in this institution that is exclusively theirs. So for some African Americans who don't get respect on the job, they can come into the church and be respected. The African American pastor must be able to deal with that freedom, ego, self-esteem, and value issues in a sensitive and yet Biblical manner without distorting the purpose of the church. In other words, it is alright for people to become respected and rise to positions of prominence in the church, but that is not the reason the church exists.

Also, the African American pastor has the privilege of leading a people who have come out of struggle and strain and who have always been committed to their churches and its leaders. Because the church has always been the center of the African American communities, the leaders of those churches have always been at the center in those communities. The following was stated by the book, *The Black Church in America:*

> The Negro preachers' stand on problems of caste and on all "political" problems is equivocal. On the one hand, he must preach "race solidarity" because his congregation demands it and because he himself stands to gain if the economic and political situation of his community improves. On the other hand, he is not only a focus of caste pressure, but his position of leadership depends upon the monopoly given him by segregation. Although the Negro preacher is "otherworldly" in his sermons, he has a closer relation to politics than has the white clergyman. In accordance with Baptist and

Methodist tenets, he preaches puritanical morals, and yet is often far from exemplary in his own life and sometimes has connections with the underworld. These paradoxes exist because the Negro preacher is not only a clergyman, but also, as Du Bois puts it, "a leader, a politician, an orator, a 'boss,' an intriguer, an idealist."[113]

This position that is enjoyed by most African American pastors in its 75,000 churches is and can be a double-edged sword depending on the character and integrity of the leader.

The view of the African American church of itself has, in some ways, changed and has, in other ways, remained the same. It has changed inasmuch as its image and esteem have been lifted. From the church have come some of the most renowned, wealthiest, and largest ministries in the country. These ministries demand and command respect from the larger society. There are large numbers of African American churches that have great economic wealth and who are changing the face of their communities. Also, some of the most educated people in the church world, in general, reside in African American churches. The view of the African American church has not changed in as much as some of the issues of the past still plague us today. Peter J. Paris makes the following observation:

> But the mission of the black churches has always transcended their own constituency by aiming at the reform of the larger white society that is,

---

[113] Nelson, *The Black Church in America*, 86-87.

causing the latter to practice racial justice as an expression of genuine Christian understanding and devotion. Their mission, therefore, has had both an internal and an external dimension in that they have sought religious, moral, and political reform in both the black and the white community, though not in the same respect.[114]

Although great strides are being made, Sunday morning worship services in our country still remain the most segregated time of the week.

The view of the larger society in respect to the African American church appears to be one of mixed emotions. The African American population makes up, by some estimation, only 13.4% of the larger population. There are some sparing attempts to integrate and assimilate the races as it relates to churches. It is this author's opinion that both races, as a whole, are not pushing for such integration and both races in the South show signs of contentment.

Over a period of time, there has been an overall advancement. African American pastors are becoming more educated. (At least there are more opportunities for education available). There is more wealth in the African American churches than ever before. Congregations have more choices available to them in their worship experiences. The media has played a major role in allowing the larger, more advanced and more educated churches to serve as examples and role models to smaller, rural congregations and pastors. With this in mind, it is clear that

---

[114] Paris, *The Social Teaching of the Black Churches*, 111.

there is hope for all African American churches and pastors in spite of the bleakness of the past.

The final question, where do the African American church and pastor in the South go from here? Lawrence N. Jones makes the following comment about the future:

> As we look toward the future, the agenda for black churches is a complex one. The existence of the churches is not in jeopardy; they are and will continue to be for large numbers of persons the only accessible institutions that will meet their need to be affirmed in their identity and sense of belonging in both a human and a divine dimension. What is in jeopardy is the capacity of the churches to attract urban dwellers in large numbers while church programs are geared to a 19th century rural ethos.[115]

The African American pastor and church must stay true to the Bible as it relates to its message and mission. As it relates to its methods, the church and pastor must take a serious look and make a serious decision to change to ensure that it remains relevant to the community and culture that it serves.

In conclusion, currently in the South, there is still racial tension between blacks and whites, there is still healing that needs to occur for past hurts, there is still confessions that need to be made for past sins, there is still forgiveness

---

[115] Lawrence N. Jones, *The Black churches: a new agenda?*, (Christian Century 96 April 18 1979), 434-438.

that needs to be made for past offenses, and there is still restitution that needs to be made for past injustices. In spite of what still needs to be done, there is celebration for what has been done, and there is hope for what will be done. As this study is concluded, it is concluded with the knowledge that things are changing even as this writing and research are being done.

Things that are currently being done as it relates to the African American pastor in the South should be noted: churches in the South are becoming healthy and growing, churches are slowly breaking away from negative traditions that have brought harm to the churches, African American pastors are becoming more educated, the financial situation in the churches are drastically improving, and black and white churches are coming together and celebrating the Lord Jesus Christ. The above may not describe every village or every hamlet, but it is the description of some, even in the Deep South.

In a class attended during the Doctor of Ministry program at Beacon University, Dr. Ronald Cottle discussed an important point in the preaching ministry. Once the preacher does all his word studies, background studies, cultural studies, etc. he must raise the question that his audience will raise as he delivers the message. That question is "so what." I have asked this question after all the research I've done pertaining to this book: "so what." In other words, the "so what" issue is about how this information relates to me, or impacts me, or what will I do with it or about it.

This book work has impacted me in a number of ways. It has made me laugh, cry, pray, think, rededicate myself to Christ and the ministry, and most of all it has made me a better, more reflective person. Also, it has moved me to a point of action and commitment. It has inspired me to do the following: 1) pray that the Lord of the Harvest will send laborers into His vineyard, 2) share the information learned with other ministers and Christian leaders, 3) appreciate the labors and sacrifices of my forefathers, 4) teach all ethnic groups the truth of history, and 5) preach deliverance to the captives of the past, who consist of both white and black people. Finally, the unspoken and unwritten impact of this work on this author will, hopefully, be spoken and written about in future generations.

APPENDIX 1

SURVEY FORM FOR PASTORS

DISCOVERING THE UNIQUE CHALLENGES OF AFRICAN AMERICAN PASTORS OF SMALL CHURCHES IN THE SOUTH

PLEASE PRINT

General Information

Title ☐ Dr.   ☐ Pastor   ☐ Rev.   ☐ Bro.
☐ Bishop   ☐ Apostle   ☐ Senior Pastor
☐ Elder   ☐ Other, _____

Gender ☐ Male ☐ Female

Age ☐ 20-29   ☐ 30-39   ☐ 40-49
☐ 50-59   ☐ 60-69   ☐ 70+

Race   ☐African American   ☐White   ☐Hispanic
☐Other, _____

Which educational levels have you completed?
(Check All That Apply)
☐ High School Graduate   ☐ 2 years of College
☐ Bachelors Degree
☐ Masters Degree   school attended _____
☐ Doctorate Degree   school attended _____
☐ Seminary Training   school attended _____
# of years ___

Personal Information   **(O P T I O N A L)**

Name _____
Address _____
City _____ State _____ Zip _____
Phone # _____

Church Information

Denomination _____

(city) _____ (state) _____

(county) _____ (zip code) _____

Age of Church

☐ 0-5 years ☐ 5-10   ☐ 11-20   ☐ 21-30

☐ 31-49   ☐ 50-75 ☐ 75-100 ☐ 100+

Which will best describe the racial mix of your congregation?
☐ Predominantly African American
☐ Predominantly Non African American
☐ All African American
☐ All Non-African American

Yearly income level of church
☐ Less than $50,000   ☐ 401,000-500,000
☐ 51,000 –100,000   ☐ 501,000 – 1,000,000
☐ 101,000-200,000   ☐ 1,000,000+
☐ 201,000-300,000
☐ 301,000 – 400,000

General Church Worship Services Times:
☐ Weekly   ☐ Bi-Weekly   ☐ Monthly

Leadership and Vision

How long have you pastored this church?   (# Years) ____

1. Who determines what happen to the finances in your church or who establishes the budget. (CHOOSE ONLY ONE)
☐ You, the Pastor
☐ A Church Board (Board of Directors, General Directors
      Board, Governing Board, Etc.)
☐ The General Church Congregation
☐ Finance Team
☐ Other, _____

2. Who is predominantly responsible for the vision in your church? (CHOOSE ONLY ONE)
☐ You, the Pastor
☐ A Church Board (Board of Directors, General Directors Board, Governing Board, Etc.)
☐ The General Church Congregation
☐ A Group of Leaders
☐ Other, _____

Congregational Expectations

1. What are the top expectations of your congregation as it relates to your duties and responsibilities? (Rank 1 to 4: with a 1 being the highest and 4 being the lowest)

_____ Visitation of the Sick
_____ Prayer and the Study of the Word
_____ Community Involvement
_____ Counseling of Church Members

2. How much time do you spend doing the following? (Rank with 1-4: 1 where you spend the most of your time and 4 where less time is spent)

_____ Visitation of the Sick
_____ Prayer and the Study of the Word
_____ Community Involvement
_____ Counseling of Church Members

3. What are your biggest challenges as a Pastor? (Rank from 1-7: 1 being the Biggest Problem to 7 being the Least Problem)

_____ Finances to handle basic expenses of church
_____ People following leadership
_____ Commitment from church members
_____ Instability of your job as Pastor
_____ Lack of knowledge to do the job
_____ Church attendance by members of the church
_____ Other _____

4. Does <u>your</u> congregation expect you to be full-time in the near future? (Full time defined as 'you receiving your total income from the church / church activities')

☐ Yes   ☐ No   ☐ Already Full Time

Pastoral Expectations

1. Do <u>you</u> expect to be full-time with the church in the near future? (**Full time defined as 'you receiving your total income from the church / church activities'**)

    ☐ Yes   ☐ No   ☐ Already Full Time

2. Do you feel that your challenges are different as a Pastor than those of other races?

    ☐ Yes   ☐ No

3. What challenges do you feel exist, as it relates to different races?

    a. _____
    b. _____
    c. _____
    d. _____

Questions of size

1. What differences exist between those who Pastor a small church vs. those who pastor a large church (500+ attendees per service)?

    a. _____
    b. _____
    c. _____
    d. _____
    e. _____

2. What is the average weekly attendance at your:

    a. Sunday morning worship service   _____
    b. Sunday night worship service   _____
    c. Sunday school   _____
    d. Mid-week service/prayer/Bible class   _____

Miscellaneous Information

1. Are you bi-vocational, as it relates to the ministry?

    ☐ Yes   ☐ No

2. Is the ministry your primary source of income?
   ☐ Yes   ☐ No

3. How many full time (paid) staff work in your church? (Excluding yourself) ___

4. How many part-time (paid) staff? (Excluding yourself) _

Optional Church Information

Name of Church _____
E-Mail _____
Address _____
Church Phone Number _____
Web Site _____

APPENDIX 2

SURVEY FORM FOR CLASS

DISCOVERING THE UNIQUE CHALLENGES
OF AFRICAN AMERICAN PASTORS
OF SMALL CHURCHES IN THE SOUTH

PLEASE PRINT

General Information

Title
☐ Dr.   ☐ Pastor   ☐ Rev.   ☐ Bro./Sis.   ☐ Bishop
☐ Apostle   ☐ Senior Pastor   ☐ Elder
☐ Other, _____

Gender   ☐ Male   ☐ Female

Age   ☐ 20-29   ☐ 30-39   ☐ 40-49
☐ 50-59   ☐ 60-69   ☐ 70+

Race   ☐ African American   ☐ White   ☐ Hispanic
☐ Other, _____

Which educational levels have you completed?
(Check All That Apply)
☐ High School Graduate   ☐ 2 years of College
☐ Bachelors Degree   ☐ Masters Degree
☐ Doctorate Degree   ☐ Seminary Training

Church Information

Denomination
_____

_____   _____
(city)   (state)

_____   _____
(county)   (zip code)

Age of Church

☐ 0-5 years ☐ 5-10 ☐ 11-20 ☐ 21-30

☐ 31-49 ☐ 50-75 ☐ 75-100 ☐ 100+

Which will best describe the racial mix of the congregation you attend?
☐ Predominantly African American
☐ Predominantly Non African American
☐ All African American
☐ All Non-African American

Yearly income level of church

☐ Less than $50,000
☐ 51,000 –100,000
☐ 101,000-200,000
☐ 201,000-300,000
☐ 301,000 – 400,000
☐ 401,000-500,000
☐ 501,000 – 1,000,000
☐ 1,000,000+

General Church Worship Services Times:
☐ Weekly ☐ Bi-Weekly ☐ Monthly

Leadership and Vision

How long have you been a member of this church?
(# Years) ___

1. Who do you think should determine what happens to the finances in your church or who should establish the budget. **(CHOOSE ONLY ONE)**
☐ Pastor
☐ A Church Board (Board of Directors, General Directors Board, Governing Board, Etc.)
☐ The General Church Congregation
☐ Finance Team
☐ Other, _____

2. Who do you think should be responsible for the vision in your church? **(CHOOSE ONLY ONE)**
☐ Pastor
☐ A Church Board (Board of Directors, General Directors Board, Governing Board, Etc.)
☐ The General Church Congregation
☐ A Group of Leaders
☐ Other, _____

Congregational Expectations

1. What are your top expectations of your Pastor as it relates to his/her duties and responsibilities? **(Rank 1, 2, 3, 4: with a 1 being the highest and 4 being the lowest)**

_____ Visitation of the Sick

_____ Prayer and the Study of the Word

_____ Community Involvement

_____ Counseling of Church Members

2. Where do you think your Pastor spends the majority of his/her time? **(Rank 1, 2, 3, 4: 1 where you spend the most of your time and 4 where less time is spent)**

_____ Visitation of the Sick

_____ Prayer and the Study of the Word

_____ Community Involvement

_____ Counseling of Church Members

3. What do you think are your Pastor's biggest challenges?
(Rank from 1, 2, 3, 4, 5, 6, 7: 1 being the Biggest Problem
to 7 being the Least Problem)

_____ Finances to handle basic expenses of the church
_____ People following leadership
_____ Commitment from church members
_____ Instability of your job as Pastor
_____ Lack of knowledge to do the job
_____ Church attendance by members of the church
_____ Other _____

4. Do you expect your Pastor to be full-time in the near future?
(Full time defined as 'you receiving your total income
from the church / church activities')

☐ Yes ☐ No ☐ Already Full Time

Pastoral Expectations

1. Does <u>your</u> pastor expect to be full-time with the church in the near future? (Full time defined as 'you receiving your total income from the church/church activities)

☐ Yes ☐ No ☐ Already Full Time

2. Do you feel that your challenges as a church are different than those of other races?

☐ Yes ☐ No

3. What challenges do you feel exist, as it relates to another race?

a. _____
b. _____
c. _____
d. _____

Questions of size

1. What differences exist between those who attend a small church vs. those who attend a large church (500+ attendees per service)?

    a. _____

    b. _____

    c. _____

    d. _____

    e. _____

2. What is the average weekly attendance at your church:

    a. Sunday morning worship service   _____

    b. Sunday night worship service   _____

    c. Sunday school   _____

    d. Mid-week service/prayer/Bible class   _____

SELECTED BIBLIOGRAPHY

Campbell, Barry. *Smaller Churches: Healthy and Growing*. Nashville, TN: Lifeway Press, 1998.

Carroll, Jackson W. *God's Potters: Pastoral Leadership and the Shaping of Congregations*. Grand Rapids, MI.: William B. Eerdmans Publishing Company, 2006.

Chaves, Mark. *Congregations in America*. Cambridge, MA.: Harvard University Press, 2004.

Damazio, Frank. *The Making Of A Leader*. Portland, Oregon: City Bible Publishing, 1988.

Daman, Glenn. *Shepherding the Small Church*. Grand Rapids: Kregel Publications, 2002.

Douglass, Kelly Brown and Hopson, Ronald E. "Understanding the Black Church: The Dynamics of Change." *Journal of Religious Thought*.. 56/57, 2/1. Spring-Fall 2001 [journal on-line], available from http://search.epnet.com/direct.asp?an=12233630&db=rlh; Internet; accessed 23, March 2005.

Evans, Tony. *What a Way to Live: Running all of Life by the Kingdom Agenda*. Nashville: Word Publishing, 1997.

Francis, Hozell C. *Church Planting in the African American Context*. Grand Rapids, Zondervan Publishing House, 1999.

Frazier, E. Franklin. *The Negro Church in America*. New York: Schocken Books, 1973

Gadzekpo, Leonard. "The Black Church, the Civil Rights Movement, and the Future." *Journal of Religious Thought*, Vol. 53/54 Issue 2/1, p 95, 1997 [journal on-line], available from http://search.epnet.com/direct.asp?an=1857238&db=rlh; Internet accessed 23 March 2005. Graff, Jim. *A Significant Life*. Colorado Springs: Waterbrook Press, 2006.

Gremillion, J.B. *The Journal of a Southern Pastor*. Chicago: Fides Publishers Association, 1957.

Guffin, Gilbert Lee. *How to Run A Church or Guides in Church Administration*. Birmingham, Alabama: Howard College Press, 1949.

Harris, James H. *Pastoral Theology A Black-Church Perspective*. Minneapolis: Fortress Press, 1991.

Hill, Samuel S. Jr. *Southern Churches in Crisis*. Chicago: Holt, Rinehart and Winston, 1966.

Hillard, Donald, Jr. *Church Growth from an African American*

Perspective. Valley Forge, PA: Judson Press, 2006.

Holck, Manfred, Jr. *Making it on a Pastor's Pay.* Nashville. New York: Abingdon Press, 1974.

Holmes, Barbara A. *Joy Unspeakable: Contemplative Practices of the Black Church.* Minneapolis, MN: Fortress Press, 2004.

Jones, Lawrence N. "The Black Churches: A New Agenda." In Christian Century. http://newfirstsearch.oclc.org 96 April 18, 1979, p 434-438.

Kimbro, Dennis and Napoleon Hill. *Think and Grow Rich: A Black Choice.* New York: Faucet books, 1991.

Larson, Bruce. Anderson, Paul. Self, Doug. *Mastering Pastoral Care.* Portland, Oregon: Multnomah, 1990.

Lincoln, Eric C. and Lawrence H. Mamiya. *The Black Church in the African American Experience.* Durham, NC.: Duke University Press, 1990.

Lindstrom, David Edgar. *American Rural Life.* New York: The Ronald Press Company, 1948.

Macchia, Stephen A. *Becoming A Healthy Church: 10 Characteristics.* Grand Rapids, Michigan: Baker Books, 1999.

Maxwell, John C. *The 21 Irrefutable Laws of Leadership.* Nashville, TN: Thomas Nelson Publishers, 1998.

Mead, Frank S. *Handbook of Denominations in the United States.* 10th edition. Nashville, TN: Abingdon Press, 1995.

Menkart, Deborah, Alana D. Murray, Jenice L. View. *Putting the Movement Back into Civil Rights Teaching.* A publication of Teaching for Change and the Poverty & Race Research Action Council (PRRAC), 2004.

Mitchell, Henry H. *Black Preaching: The Recovery of a Powerful Art.* Nashville, TN: Abingdon Press, 1990.

_____. *Black Church Beginnings.* Grand Rapids, Michigan: William B. Eerdmans Publishing Company, 2004.

Moyd, Olin P. *The Sacred Art: Preaching and Theology in the African American Tradition.* Valley Forge, PA.: Judson Press, 1995.

Nelson, Hart, et al., eds *The Black Church in America.* New York: Basic Books, Inc., 1971.

Paris, Peter J. *The Social Teaching of the Black Churches.* Philadelphia: Fortress Press, 1985.

Pinn, Anthony B. *The Black Church in the Post-Civil Rights Era.*

Maryknoll, NY: Orbis Books, 2002.

Pinn, Anne H. and Anthony B. Pinn. *Black Church History.* Minneapolis, MN: Fortress Press, 2002.

Roosevelt, Robinson, Jr. *A People Risen Up Out Of Struggle; The History of the Black Baptist Church.* A research paper presented to the Faculty of the Graduate School of Florida Beacon College, 1981.

Simmons, Charitey. "Leaders for Black Churches." In Christian Century. http://web15.epnet.com/direct.asp?an=9502205665&db=rlh 1 February 95, Volume 112 Issue 4, p100.

Smith, Wallace Charles. *The Church in the Life of the Black Family.* Valley Forge, PA: Judson Press, 1985.

Taylor, Lee and Jones, Arthur R. *Rural Life and Urbanized Society.* New York: Oxford University Press, 1964.

Thiessen, John C. *Pastoring the Smaller Church: A Complete and Comprehensive Guidebook for Pastors.* Grand Rapids, Michigan: Zondervan Publishing House, 1962.

Wagner, C. Peter. *Church Growth State of the Art.* Wheaton: Tyndale House, 1986.

Warren, Rick. *The Purpose Driven Church.* Grand Rapids, Michigan: Zondervan Publishing House, 1995.

Washington, Joseph R. Jr. *The Politics of God: The Future of the Black Churches.* Boston: Beacon Press, 1967.

_____. *Black Religion: The Negro and Christianity in the United States.* Boston: Beacon Press, 1964.

Webster'sTower Dictionary. Cleveland: The World Publishing Company, 1955.

White, Daniel III. *When Black Preachers Preach.* Atlanta, GA: Torch Publications, 1994.

Woods, Paul. *Great Preaching: Practical Advice from Powerful Preachers.* Group Publishing Inc. Loveland, Co., 2003.

Woodson, Carter G. and Charles H. Wesley, *The Negro In Our History*, (Washington, D.C.: Associated Publishers, 1962), 1966.

World Book Encyclopedia. World Book, Inc. a Scott Fetzer Company: Chicago 1999.

ABOUT THE AUTHOR

Dr. Terry L. Weems, a native of Laurel, MS, is a graduate of Christian Life School of Theology (Doctor of Ministry) and Beacon University (Doctor of Ministry). He is Senior Pastor of New Life Fellowship Churches, with locations in Columbia (1988), McComb (1997), and Silver Creek (2004), MS. He is Chancellor and an instructor of the New Life Fellowship School of Ministry and also serves as Overseer of the A.C.T.S. Fellowship of Pastors and Ministry Leaders, which he founded.

Pastor Weems is a community leader, businessman, mentor and author who travels frequently, preaching and teaching the Word of God with excitement and destiny, giving a life-inspiring Word with a realization that you have "*One Life to Live*".

Terry and his wife Sherry W. Hines Weems are parents of two sons, T.J. (Destinie) and the late J.T. (2003-2003) who graced this side of glory for 27 days before going to be with the Lord. The Weems family resides in Columbia, MS.

www.TerryLWeems.com

Available in the United States and Europe
Available in print and digitally on Amazon.com

www.ingramcontent.com/pod-product-compliance
Lightning Source LLC
Chambersburg PA
CBHW020917090426
42736CB00008B/667